Obedience

A Journey of Love

Beverlin Hammett

ISBN-13: 978-1530134885

ISBN-10: 1530134889

Ordering Information:
Quantity sales. Special discounts are available on quantity purchases by corporations, associations, and others. For details, contact the publisher at info@3lsglobal.org

Orders by U.S. trade bookstores and wholesalers. Please contact 3LS Global Inc.
email: info@3lsglobal.org

Scripture quotations marked NIV are taken from the Holy Bible, New International Version. NIV. Copyright 1973, 1978, 1984 by International Bible Society. Used by permission of Zondervan. All rights reserved.

Scripture quotations marked NKJV are taken from the New King James Version. Copyright 1982 by Thomas Nelson, Inc. Used by permission. All rights reserved.

Scripture quotations marked MSG are taken from The Message. Copyright 1993, 1994, 1995, 1996, 2000, 2001, 2002, 2003 by Eugene H. Peterson. Used by permission of NavPress Publishing Group.

Printed in the United States of America

1 2 3 4 5 6 7 —13 12 11 10 9 8

Contents

Dedication

I dedicate this book to everyone I have met during this journey.
Those who are running this amazing race with Christ and those who
are just beginning to crawl.

May your love for Jesus Christ be seen throughout the earth.

The Journey Begins

And this is love:

That we walk in obedience to his commands.

As you have heard from the beginning,

his command is that you walk in love.

(2 John 1:6)

Obedience:

An Active Display of Love

As I sit here in Israel overlooking Jerusalem, I cannot help but reflect on the first time I was told that I should write a book. It was after I had returned from a tour through various parts of South East Asia during my late 20s. Since then, I have received countless prophetic words from Christians and advice from non-Christians concerning the number of books that I should, and would eventually write to share all that has transpired during my years of being in love with Jesus.

I did not realize that I would be putting the final touches on *Obedience: A Journey of Love*, my first book, while traveling to two places that captured my heart years ago, Paris, France and various parts of Israel, especially, Bethlehem. When God gave me the directive to have the book finished, I felt I needed to finish it by February 14th, 2016. This date represents Valentine's Day in some countries, and given such, I realized that I was entering a new realm of understanding God's love.[1]

Since meeting Jesus on an airplane, I have often prayed, "Jesus, I want to love others the way you love me." This is not the, "I need to know more of God's love," or the "I need to receive God's love for me," that I sadly hear so many Christians pray. When I met Him, the love that He had and has for me was 100% clear. I knew that the love I was given, was the love I was loving Him back with. You see, we can't simply love God in our own natural strength. We can only love Him by willingly receiving Jesus Christ, who is love, who empowers us to love Him, and love God with the love we have been given.

Asking God to help me fully understand how I could actively, as one with Him, love others, has put me in various precarious situations in a number of different nations. I have encountered people who not only needed to know that they were made in His image, but they also needed to know that they were loved by Him.

For those who have written a book, or even a number of books, you and I know that the most challenging part of writing is wanting to write what we believe God desires for us to share with those who will honor us with their time. I use the word 'honor' because time is the number one commodity that is priceless and can't be duplicated. Given such, I thank you in advance for taking the time to even pick up this book to consider reading it.

---

[1] Each year on February 14th, many people exchange cards, candy, gifts or flowers with their special "valentine." Valentine's Day, also called Saint Valentine's Day or the Feast of Saint Valentine, is an annual holiday celebrated on February 14. It originated as a Western Christian liturgical feast day honoring one or more early saints named Valentinus, and is recognized as a significant cultural and commercial celebration in many regions around the world, although it is not a public holiday in any country. Several martyrdom stories associated with the various Valentines that were connected to February 14 were added to later martyrologies, including a popular hagiographical account of Saint Valentine of Rome which indicated he was imprisoned for performing weddings for soldiers who were forbidden to marry and for ministering to Christians, who were persecuted under the Roman Empire. According to legend, during his imprisonment, Saint Valentine healed the daughter of his jailer, Asterius, and before his execution, he wrote her a letter signed "Your Valentine" as a farewell.

The next challenging part of writing is recapping all of your thoughts, encounters, emails, letters, and testimonies to put them all together, where the reader will not only have a glimpse into your life, but most importantly encounter God in a special, and hopefully a new way.

Obedience: A Journey of Love not only details some adventures that I have had with God, but it will also have stories of some of the most amazing people I have encountered over the years. The stories are about being obedient to God's call to do, go, give, and willingly obey all that He requires to love, help, serve, and honor others.

I had no idea how these stories should be ordered. I pondered whether the stories should be written chronologically or should they be written in a manner where similar stories are grouped together. Contemplating how the stories should be ordered was one of the reasons it took some time to start putting these testimonies together. I am not sure why I did not immediately think that God would guide me as I wrote. But as I began, He brought back memories of testimonies and guided me in various ways as to how the stories should be organized.

Within a few minutes of typing out the first story, He and in His amazing way of doing things gave me a strategy as to how to put the stories together. From a baby learning to walk, to an adult running a marathon, *Obedience: A Journey of Love* will take you on a journey that is likened to a baby learning how to crawl, toddle, fall, walk, and then eventually run.

I began writing while in South Korea. It was during a week where yet another threat was coming in from North Korea. While writing, I kept thinking about Paris. I figured it had to do with the fact that for almost a year, I, along with another friend, would see the word 'Paris' or the Eiffel Tower in the strangest places. On a wall, on someone's bag, on a wrapper on the street, in an ad, on a tee shirt, or even someone mentioning Paris in a conversation…EVERYDAY. Given all of the Paris related sightings, we simply knew it was God highlighting the city. Due to the fact that it was happening every day, we would take a picture of what we saw, and send it to each other. While walking, if we saw someone with an item that had a reference to Paris, we would either stop the person and ask to take a picture of the item, or, proceed as 'paparazzi' and take a picture as the individual whizzed by. I knew God desired for us to pray for Paris, while also knowing that eventually He desired for us to visit the city, *The City of Lights*.

God did send my friend for a week, and she had a marvelous time. However, one day, in mid-November, after spending the day writing, I went to sleep with Paris heavy on my mind. The next morning I woke up and googled Paris. To my shock, all of the news outlets were covering the terrorist attack that had occurred the day before. I had no idea as to what had happened being that I do not have a television and do not have direct access to English newspapers, unless I am lead to access them online. As I read the headlines, I clearly heard God say, "Now go to Paris!" It was after hearing that I should go to Paris, I was able to book my plane ticket in order to join a team that was already scheduled to go to Israel.

At the end of December, I had completed writing this book and sent it to a company for editing. But there were issues with the company, and I found myself in mid-January searching for an independent editor. Within two weeks, the editor sent back the book, but it was the same day I was leaving for Paris. I thought this book would be in print by the 14th of February, but that was not the case. I realized that I would be putting the finishing touches on the book, and editing this section, while in France, Israel, and Palestine, and eventually completing it on February 14th, while in Paris Charles de Gaulle Airport waiting for my flight back to South Korea.

Even as I was making additional edits, first while sitting in a hotel in Paris and then while in a Palestinian refugee camp in Bethlehem, and now in Jerusalem, I realized that the journey I have been on with God is an answer to my prayers of wanting to have revelation of His love for people around the world, especially those who are in conflict with one other.

It is no coincidence that this book has been written and edited while in nations that are: (a) technically still at war, South and North Korea are in a state of a ceasefire given the Korean Armistice Agreement (b) suffering from unresolved conflict, Israelis and Palestinians are still fighting to resolve issues associated with security, water rights, control of Jerusalem, Israeli settlements, Palestinian freedom of movement, Palestinian right of return, or; (c) dealing with terrorist attacks, shootings and bombings by terrorist groups in Paris.

We must understand that God is not surprised by conflict. However, He does desire for nations and individuals that have conflict to have regard for humanity. I cannot and will not understand, no matter how many people I talk to, who try to explain, why individuals will not only kill themselves, but hurt or kill others in the name of achieving political, economic, or social freedom, or even domination.

During the weeks in Israel and Palestine, I had what looked like 'heated' arguments with individuals that I completely disagreed with. But, because of my desire to understand and honor those that I did not agree with, I made sure that they were clear that I truly wanted to understand their position, and not determine if they were right or wrong. Due to this, they not only saw that I desired to honor them during the discussions, but they felt it as well. I even found myself in tears as an Arab widow stood up in order to plant kisses on my face, after angrily yelling at me in response to a question that I had a translator ask.

My interactions with this widow were possible because I was serving with a Christian group that I was a part of who were serving Arab widows and orphans by bringing hugs, joy, toys and food. There were widows who joined in the fun by laughing and dancing. However, I noticed three widows who were clearly angry as they sat with their arms crossed and did not want anyone to hug them or shake their hands.

As I stood next to them, praying for God to capture their hearts, I asked for a translator to ask them, "What do you think about all of this, and please be honest?" One of the widows started yelling, "What is all of this when our husbands and sons are dead..." She said some other things along these lines, and after she had finished, I told the translator to thank her for her honesty.

The translator walked away, but I continued to stand next to these women who were still very angry and unimpressed. However, within five minutes of the translator walking away, the widow who did the yelling, stood up, limped over to me, kissed both of my cheeks and hugged me. I lost it! Tears started to stream down my face as I hugged her. As she kissed my tears, it was at that moment she turned around to the other two widows and said something. They began to smile while shaking their heads up and down in agreement with what she said while pointing at me.

From that point on, I continued to stand next to them during our visit. I also noticed after our exchange, when the next person came by to reach out to them, they extended their hands to allow them to be shaken. After that first shake, they looked at me, smiled, and I, still through tears, smiled back indicating that I was okay, because they were okay.

It was at that moment in time that I realized even more that the feelings I always felt for those who were angry, for good or bad reasons, were God's compassion and His desire to take the pain that they felt away in order for them to feel and know His love.

One must realize that the only emotion that will last for eternity is love. Why? Because God is love. And when His creation, whether they know Him or not, have emotions like rage, jealousy, and a host of others, the desire He has for them, should grow even more inside of us who carry His presence, who carry His glory, who represent Him here in the earth realm.

Do you not know that you are a temple of God and that the Spirit of God dwells in you? (1 Corinthians 3:16)

Knowing that the Spirit of God, the Holy Spirit dwells in us, is the only way that we can do all that He requires of us, and that is to love Him with all our heart, mind, and strength, while also loving others. (Matthew 22:37-38)

But, most Christians do not realize that we cannot say we love Him and disobey Him. When one says that it is hard for them to forgive, to love, to be obedient, to walk in freedom, it is these individuals who have yet to come into the revelation that it is simply a *decision* that needs to be made to believe His word...and obey it. The process of walking out His word is the part where we use our free will, in conjunction with the power He has given us, to take each step.

Jesus answered and said to him, "If anyone loves Me, he will keep My word; and My Father will love him, and We will come to him and make Our abode with him. (John 14:23)

Knowing the One who resides in you is the only way you will walk in obedience. Actually, having revelation of this truth is the only way you would want to obey Him. It is my heart's desire that as you read this book, you not only enjoy the testimonies, but you would truly understand that you have been empowered to love Him and joyously obey Him.

If you picked this book up for yourself, or for a friend, allow me to tell you what you will be giving your time to.

First, each part of the six sections start out with an excerpt from the Bible that I believe coincides with the testimonies you will read. When I was first told to write a book, I remember saying, "**People need to spend more time reading the Bible and not stories about my escapades with the Lord.**" I thought, why would someone read a story about a woman they did not know? Then I realized that the first thought had to do with 'me'. However, the purpose of any book written by a Christian should always be about *Him*.

After I got past the 'me' hurdle, also known as *pride*, the next thought I had was, why would someone want to read about my adventures, which I alone with Jesus cherished, when they should definitely consider reading more of the classics such as St. Athanasius *On the Incarnations*, which is considered an apologetic treatise. St. Athanasius defends the incarnation of Christ against the derision of 4th-century non-believers. St Athanasius explains why God chose to approach His fallen people in human form. He states:

"You must understand why it is that the Word of the Father, so great and so high, has been made manifest in bodily form. He has not assumed a body as proper to His own nature, far from it, for as the Word He is without body. He has been manifested in a human body for this reason only, out of the love and goodness of His Father, for the salvation of us men."[2]

Along with St. Athanasius, you have Saint Augustine of Hippo, an early Church Father and Doctor of the Church. A famous passage from St. Augustine's *Confessions* states "You have made us for yourself, O Lord, and our heart is restless until it rests in you."[3]

How about C.S. Lewis, *Mere Christianity*? I believe that every Christian should have read at least one of C.S. Lewis' many works. If I were to recommend one, it would be *Mere Christianity*. "The real Son of God is at your side. He is beginning to turn you into the same kind of thing as Himself. He is beginning, so to speak, to inject His kind of life and thought, His Zoe, into you; he is beginning to turn the tin soldier into a live man. The part of you that does not like it is the part that is still tin."[4] If you can't say "Amen!", say "Ouch!"

I hope those words propelled you to lay back and ponder the depths in which God loves us. But before moving on, I need to also recommend, *The Cost of Discipleship* by Dietrich Bonhoeffer:

"Cheap grace is the preaching of forgiveness without requiring repentance, baptism without church discipline, Communion without confession, absolution without personal confession. Cheap grace is grace without discipleship, grace without the cross, and grace without Jesus Christ, living and incarnate. Costly grace is... the call of Jesus Christ at which the disciple leaves his nets and follows him... Such grace is costly because it calls us to follow, and it is grace because it calls us to follow Jesus Christ. It is

---

[2]Saint Athanasius, *St. Athanasius on the incarnation: The treatise De Incarnatione Verbi Dei* (London: A.R. Mowbray & Co. 1963), chapter 1
[3]Saint Aurelius Augustin: Bishop of Hippo The Confessions of St. Augustine In Thirteen Books Translated and Annotated by J.G. Pilkington, M.A., (Lib 1,1-2,2.5,5: CSEL 33, 1-5)
[4]C.S. Lewis, Mere Christianity (1952; Harper Collins: 2001) 189.

costly because it costs a man his life, and it is grace because it gives a man the only true life."[5]

After Ten Years. Letters and Papers from Prison

"Who stands firm? Only the one for whom the final standard is not his reason, his principles, his conscience, his freedom, his virtue, but who is ready to sacrifice all these, when in faith and sole allegiance to God he is called to obedient and responsible action: the responsible person, whose life will be nothing but an answer to God's question and call."[6]

After reading a number of masterpieces, it was easy for me to think that I did not have a lot to say. But, I had to realize, yet again, that those thoughts about the great writers were still based on thoughts about 'me', and that is when I knew that I wasn't ready to share the stories you are about to read.

When I grasped that there are so many facets of how Jesus shows His love to each and every one of us, *uniquely*, and how He shares His love with us so that we can share it with others, I knew then that He chose me to have these encounters with Him. Not because I am better than anyone else, but because I am His one and only beloved. Just like *YOU* are His One and only beloved.

You see, when Jesus shared with the disciples in John 14 that we should obey Him because we love Him, He is not telling us, *"I know you love me, because you obey me."* He is telling us, that we are truly His when we obey Him, and we obey Him because we love Him.

I do believe that this is one thing that non-Christians and Christian alike get mixed up. Obeying Jesus in not like obeying your Staff Sargent in the military. It is not even similar to obeying your teacher when they tell you to do something in school. Obeying Him is like obeying our parents, because when they tell us to do something, while we are young, it is because they love us and know the outcome of our actions long

---

[5]Bonhoeffer, Dietrich. *The Cost of Discipleship.* New York: Macmillan, 1966
[6]Bonhoeffer, Dietrich. "After Ten Years." *Letters and Papers from Prison.* Enlarged Edition, Eberhard Bethge, ed. New York: The Macmillan Company, 1971, p. 5.

before we do. And because we love them and know that they love us, we listen and obey when they tell us not to touch the hot stove. Some people however, do touch the hot stove… figuratively and literally.

Even though we can think of times our parents told us not to do something, we now know that it was for our best interest. But one of the many differences between obeying our parents and obeying Jesus is that He is in us, and He empowers us with His grace and love to obey Him. How does the Holy Spirit empower obedience?

Answering that question will take another book on being filled with and being led by the Holy Spirit,[7] who empowers up all to live right. However, we have to keep in mind that we do not harvest the power of the Holy Spirit in order to *use* God. We experience His power when we surrender to Him and are consistently led by the Holy Spirit. God empowers us with His power as we walk in obedience to Him. When we make a decision to walk in love, it is His love that He gives for us to love Him back and love others. *19 We love because he first loved us. 20 Whoever claims to love God yet hates a brother or sister is a liar. For whoever does not love their brother and sister, whom they have seen, cannot love God, whom they have not seen. (1John 4:19-20)*

It is His love that we received, that empowers us to love Him and others. We do not have love in us without the One who is love. Yes, there is a worldly love that is shared between individuals, that is either learned from our family and/or society. But God is love (1John 4:8,16).

When we surrender our life to the One who created everything, both seen and unseen, He accepts our 'Yes' to His invitation to give us a life that we cannot fathom. He then dwells within us. And because He dwells within us, we love Him back with the love that is purely and totally Him.

If you choose to obey God without the power of who He is in us, the Holy Spirit sent by Jesus, then you can glorify yourself and say, "YOU obeyed God," and mistakenly believe that He owes something for your obedience. But, when you obey Him because of the love you have in you, which is Jesus Christ himself, it is God in you that

---

[7]Ephesians 5:18, Acts 6:3, Exodus 31:3, Luke 1:15

is interacting and following the path that was laid out for you before time began.

Take a minute and think about it, when you read about the 'fruit' of the Spirit, *love, joy, peace, patience, goodness, kindness, faithfulness, gentleness, and self-control, which reveal the character of Christ in us*, it is Him in us that we are displaying. (Galatians 5:22-23). These fruits that should manifest in every Christian represents Him. Actually, the only part you have to do, initially, is choose to receive Him. And in your choosing to line up your free-will with Him, you cannot live a life without bursting forth ultimate bliss due to knowing that you said 'Yes' to the One who not only created you, but has chosen you to represent Him for those who know Him, those who have yet to come to know Him, or even better, represent Him for those who want nothing to do with Him.

You will also read stories about what it means to 'obey', not just His commands spelled out in His word, but obey His voice as He leads you to do, and become all that He has destined. You will also, I hope, laugh at the antics that one goes through when 'learning' to hear His voice. And lastly, this is my deepest desire for anyone who reads this book, that you will walk on water without looking to your left, your right, or down, to run the race He has set out for you. All while developing a deeper love for the One who is *love*.

The scriptures are alive with testimonies of those who walked in obedience and those who did not. While reading the Word, I thought about all the kings in 2nd Chronicles. When was the last time you read 2nd Chronicles? An even better question, when was the last time you read 2nd Chronicles and wondered, "What was it going to take for the Israelites to simply trust and worship God?" How many times did they need to be in captivity, or suffer the consequences of disobeying God?

Then I realized that I wasn't disappointed with how the hearts of the Israelites so easily turned to their 'high places' which were idols, but how easy it was for me to turn to my own 'high places' of complacency in not reading the Word as much as I used to.

Please do not misinterpret the above statement. Reading the Word for hours a day for some is considered impressive. But when you know, you have a history of reading the Word for at least three to four hours a day, but now find yourself only reading two hours a day because your desire is waning, only you and God know that there is an issue that needs to be addressed.

While thinking about the Israelites and their kings, I thought about searching for a graph or chart of all the kings and their descendants. As I was looking for a chart, I wondered, "Who was the first king of Israel". Yes, I knew that it was Saul, but for some reason, I did not automatically recall that Saul was the first king chosen for the Israelites.

Then, I began to search using a Bible software that I had received as a gift from a friend. While looking up the king's name, it occurred to me that "Saul was the first king of Israel" and he, of course, did not end well. But what is the name of the man who wrote most of the books of the New Testament that give us insight into who we are in God and how to walk with Him? His name was Saul but changed to Paul. Why did I not realize this before? Why was that connection something that escaped my understanding given the fact that I like to see how the Bible connects everything, from Genesis to Revelation?[8]

The name Saul means, 'Prayed For'. The meaning of the name is significant because the children of Israel asked God for a king and Saul was His immediate answer to them. King Saul was not born a king, and neither was Saul of Tarsus born an apostle. Both men were from the tribe of Benjamin, and both of them were called by God to become something special. In one's case, it was to become the first king of Israel, and in the others, it was to become an apostle.

They both had similar characteristics, but at different points in time. When Saul was anointed, he was humble, but it was his pride that contributed to God despising him. While King Saul had pride, in the end, Saul of Tarsus' pride, in the beginning, caused him to retaliate

---

[8]The Bible was written over a period of roughly 2,000 years by 40 different authors from three continents, who wrote in three different languages. Despite writing in radically different times and contexts, the Bible's many authors all told the same message about God's eternal plan, from Creation and the Flood to Christ's work on the Cross and the consummation of God's plan. You can find the same truths stated by Moses and the Old Testament prophets, Christ Himself, and Christ's apostles.

against God. His pride had blinded him so much that he could not see that he was fighting with God. When God opened his eyes, pride fell from him, and humility took over. He was able to walk in the will of God and was obedient because he no longer had pride.

Only the humble will obey God. Given all of the stories we have read in the Bible, only the humble will consistently hear and see Him in order to obey Him.

Also, as I was researching the Kings' lists, I came across Beville, K. (2004). *Exploring Ezra: The Secret of Spiritual Success.* The book is about leadership, and it mentioned Ezra, which is the next book I was about to read, prior to doing my research on Saul. I know that some of you can relate, but don't you love the way God leads you as you seek to know more of Him. It is like a teacher taking your hand and walking you through the library of knowledge, and you are amazed at all the wonderful things you discovered. *2 It is the glory of God to conceal a matter; to search out a matter is the glory of kings. 3 As the heavens are high and the earth is deep, so the hearts of kings are unsearchable. (Proverbs 25:2-3)*

As I was reading, I discovered the following:

"...An active trust in the Lord will result in God's plans being prospered. Trust demands courage and courage, in turn, is a noble virtue. In the educational system of bygone days, people of history were held up as examples of noble character. The same is true of heroes in literature who were seen as role models for students who were being trained in character as well as intellect. Ezra is a man from whom we can learn a great deal. We can derive lessons in leadership from this great hero of history. One of the essential lessons we learn is that our trust in God will never be disappointed. It is most likely that Ezra learned to trust the Lord as he grew from spiritual infancy to maturity of faith. **Our growth in the spiritual life is like that of the physical realm where children usually learn to crawl before taking baby steps. As**

they grow in confidence, they learn to toddle and eventually to walk and run."[9]

Why is the above so amazing? I previously shared, that I had prayed for God to help me write in the order He wanted. As He guided me, I realized that this book was to be written in association with how one develops the ability to crawl, walk, and then run. And here is K. Beville, writing about growing in the Lord, and moving from infancy to maturity in our faith.

I pray that as you read the words on the following pages, you develop a deeper trust in God. That the scriptures come alive to you as it relates to being wise and not foolish, walking in peace and not chaos, and living in a consistent state of love and joy for yourself, and for those around you. How is this done? By simply walking in obedience to Him, and walking alongside others who are also going in 'His' direction.

*Matthew 7:24 "Therefore everyone who hears these words of mine and puts them into practice is like a **wise man** who built his house on the rock. 25 The rain came down, the streams rose, and the winds blew and beat against that house; **yet it did not fall, because it had its foundation on the rock.** 26 But everyone who hears these words of mine and does not put them into practice is like a foolish man who built his house on sand. 27 The rain came down, the streams rose, and the winds blew and beat against that house, and it fell with a great crash."*

May you know that even though you are steadfast in your walk in obedience to Him, storms may come, but you will not be over-taken. Be aware that when the winds of adversity seem to be overwhelming, keep your mind focused on Jesus because that is when you will have perfect peace.

---

[9] K. Beville. *Exploring Ezra: the secret of spiritual success* (Leominster, UK: Day One Publications 2004), p. 131.

I also hope that you will develop more questions about Jesus, where you can boldly pray and seek Him...for Him. And, may you find yourself in step with our Father, walking fully submitted to His perfect will, obeying His Word and most importantly, letting Him love you so that you can not only feel loved, but love all those you encounter.

Crawling

The Fall of Man

3 Now the serpent was more cunning than any beast of the field which the Lord God had made. And he said to the woman, "Has God indeed said, 'You shall not eat of every tree of the garden'?" 2 And the woman said to the serpent, "We may eat the fruit of the trees of the garden; 3 but of the fruit of the tree which is in the midst of the garden, God has said, 'You shall not eat it, nor shall you touch it, lest you die.'" 4 Then the serpent said to the woman, "You will not surely die. 5 For God knows that in the day you eat of it your eyes will be opened, and you will be like God, knowing good and evil." 6 So when the woman saw that the tree was good for food, that it was pleasant to the eyes, and a tree desirable to make one wise, she took of its fruit and ate. She also gave to her husband with her, and he ate. 7 Then the eyes of both of them were opened, and they knew that they were naked; and they sewed fig leaves together and made themselves coverings.

8 And they heard the sound of the Lord God walking in the garden in the cool of the day, and Adam and his wife hid themselves from the presence of the Lord God among the trees of the garden. 9 Then the Lord God called to Adam and said to him, "Where are you?" 10 So he said, "I heard Your voice in the garden, and I was afraid because I was naked; and I hid myself."

11 And He said, "Who told you that you were naked? Have you eaten from the tree of which I commanded you that you should not eat?" 12 Then the man said, "The woman whom You gave to be with me, she gave me of the tree, and I ate." 13

And the Lord God said to the woman, "What is this you have done?" The woman said, "The serpent deceived me, and I ate."

14 So the Lord God said to the serpent:

"Because you have done this, You are cursed more than all cattle, And more than every beast of the field; On your belly you shall go, And you shall eat dust all the days of your life. 15 And I will put enmity between you and the woman, and between your seed and her Seed; He shall bruise your head, And you shall bruise His heel."

16 To the woman He said:

"I will greatly multiply your sorrow and your conception; In pain you shall bring forth children; your desire shall be for your husband, and he shall rule over you." 17 Then to Adam He said, "Because you have heeded the voice of your wife, and have eaten from the tree of which I commanded you, saying, 'You shall not eat of it': "Cursed is the ground for your sake; in toil you shall eat of it all the days of your life. 18 Both thorns and thistles it shall bring forth for you, and you shall eat the herb of the field. 19 In the sweat of your face you shall eat bread till you return to the ground, for out of it you were taken; for dust you are, and to dust you shall return."

20 And Adam called his wife's name Eve, because she was the mother of all living. 21 Also for Adam and his wife the Lord God made tunics of skin, and clothed them.

22 Then the Lord God said, "Behold, the man has become like one of Us, to know good and evil. And now, lest he put out his hand and take also of the tree of life, and eat, and live forever"— 23 therefore the Lord God sent him out of the garden of Eden to till the ground from which he was taken. 24 So He drove out the man; and He placed cherubim at the east of the Garden of Eden, and a flaming sword which turned every way, to guard the way to the tree of life. (Genesis 3:3-24). [10]

It is clear from the start that Adam and Eve lived together in a perfect paradise, the Garden of Eden, until they disobeyed God by eating fruit from the Tree of the Knowledge of Good and Evil. That

[10]Scripture taken from the New King James Version®. Copyright © 1982 by Thomas Nelson. Used by permission. All rights reserved.

act of sin, defiance, and disobedience, called "The Fall" is the reason for our separation from God, painful childbirth, weeds in our garden, and ultimately death. Moreover, Adam and Eve's disobedience not only gave death the right to have power, but it initiated fear and alienation into humankind's formerly perfect relationships with God, and between one another.

Having once walked freely with Him, and now being afraid of him due to receiving knowledge of good and evil, all mankind would be forever changed, until a Savior was born.

We do not know what it was like for Adam and Eve to walk and exist in perfect union with God prior to their disobedience to Him. However, one needs to contemplate, was it an act of obedience while communing with Him, or a simple act of being one with the One who created them. Given the fact that they did, 'disobey', we now have to ponder, how then can we walk in obedience to God?

There are two ways to approach walking in obedience: you can approach it as, "Aye-aye Sir[11], or Roger Wilco[12], I will obey your every command." Or, you can receive the guidance He provides through the Holy Spirit because He loves you and will not lead you astray.

Unfortunately, I have encountered a number of Christians who started out, and sadly, for years, approached walking in obedience to God as if they were a low-ranking soldier in the military, who simply followed orders. Some even see Him as a dictator who has an agenda,

---

[11]"Aye-aye, Sir" is a phrase commonly heard present day in naval language. It is derived from a duplicate of the word "aye" which came into the English language in the late 16th century and early 17th century, meaning "Yes; even so. Aye aye' ie 'Yes yes' means *'Yes I understand your order'* and *'Yes I will follow your order'*. Oxford English Dictionary. "Aye Aye". Oxford English Dictionary. Retrieved 19 December 2015

[12] "Roger" was "phonetic" for "R" (received and understood". In radio communication, a "spelling alphabet" (often mistakenly called a "phonetic alphabet) is used to avoid confusion between similarly sounding letters. In the previously used US spelling alphabet, R was Roger, which in radio voice procedure means "Received". While in the current spelling alphabet (NATO), R is now Romeo, Roger has remained the response meaning "received" in radio voice procedure. In the US military, it is common to reply to another's assertion with "Roger Wilco", meaning: "Received, I will Comply,". During Navy training, ROGER stands for Received Order Given, Expect Results.

and that agenda is 'self-serving'. All of which have nothing to do with who God is and who we are to Him.

Have you ever questioned, "Why did Adam and Eve sin?" We know 'how they sinned', but I have often contemplated, why and how would they sin without having a sinful nature? Being that God created them, they were made perfect, in His image. And yet, they still chose to disobey.

Some people would ask the question by presenting it as such, *"If Adam and Eve were made in God's image, how could they choose to sin?"* By using the word 'if', it presents an accusation that provides doubt to the truth that they were made in God's image. And some even go as far to propagate, if there is a God, why would He create them to sin? Which would lead one to compose an answer that would identify God himself as the author of sin.

One needs to be sure that they understand 'The Fall', but more so, understand all that happened before, during and after the fall. Why you might ask?

First, if you believe that God created Adam and Eve with a sinful nature, then you could go through life thinking, 'if Adam and Eve disobeyed God, why would and could God expect me to obey Him'?

Secondly, if Adam and Eve sinned without a sinful nature, that would mean that God did not create them perfect. And if God did not create them perfect, then why would God expect me to be perfect and walk in His ways, given the fact that I am a descendant of Adam?

Thirdly, if God made them in his image, what exactly does that mean? And if their image was that of God, does God have sin in Him, which would explain why they were able to sin?

All of these questions are ones that you must answer for yourself. It should not be a situation where you come up with answers to fit your theology in order to justify your state of sin or feelings of insignificance. Tozer said, "God will conform to the image of the one who created it and will be considered cruel or kind, according to the moral state of the mind from which it emerges. A god begotten in the shadows of a fallen heart will quite naturally be no true likeness of the true God."[13]

These questions should propel you to seek out the truth in the Word to determine, who is this God you claim to serve and love.

Tozer said:

"The man who comes to a right belief about God is relieved of 10,000 temporal problems, for he sees at once that these have to do with matters that at the most cannot concern him for very long; but even if the multiple burdens of time may be lifted from him, the one mighty single burden of eternity begins to press down upon him with a weight more crushing than all the woes of the world piled one upon another. That mighty burden is his obligation to God. It includes an instant and lifelong duty to love God with every power of mind and soul, to obey Him perfectly, and to worship Him acceptably. And when the man's laboring conscience tells him that he has done none of these things, but has from childhood been guilty of foul revolts against the Majesty in the heavens, the inner pressure of self-accusation may become too heavy to bear.

The gospel can lift this destroying burden from the mind, give beauty for ashes, and the garment of praise for the spirit of heaviness. But unless the weight of the burden is felt, the gospel can mean nothing to the man; and until he sees a vision of God high and lifted up, there will be no woe and no burden. Low views of God destroys the gospel for all who hold them."[14]

Since meeting Jesus, I now know that all of the encounters that I have had during my time of loving and walking with Him were, and still, are associated with increasing my knowledge of who He is. It is my hope that you discover that loving Him is the only way you will lovingly, and not begrudgingly, obey Him. Having faith in the one and only *One*

---

[13] A. W. Tozer. *The knowledge of the holy: The attributes of God: their meaning in the Christian life*. (Harrisburg, Pa: Christian Publications, 1961), 5
[14] Ibid. pg. 5-6

who has a plan for your life, is the only way you too can have a journey of love.

Staying On Wall Street

For anyone who has held a newborn baby, we all know that one thing is consistent; they all kick and stretch their little chubby legs. Their legs aren't strong enough to support themselves, but if you hold them upright under their arms, they instinctively push up and down, against the surface of your thighs or chest with their feet, almost as if they know that their feet are made for walking. After about five months, they are in the bouncy stage, where they bounce up and down when held in a standing position. This movement helps babies build leg strength.

Like a baby, God treats us as a good father would, He holds us, coddles us, and pretty much does everything for us, as we begin our new life with him. When we are born again, the Lord is so loving, kind, and tender to us. This is not to say that He isn't as we grow, but it is similar to how a father is to a newborn child.

I am not sure about you, but like a baby, I cried and cried often. I cried when I felt the love of our Father, I cried when I saw Him loving others. I would sit and read the Bible and simply weep at His goodness. It's interesting that a newborn baby enters the world crying, and new

born-again believers, normally cry when they are, well born again. I believe it is important to explain how I came to the realization that Jesus Christ is real.

I encountered Jesus while on a plane, flying from Nigeria, via London, to New York City. I was not searching for God, nor did I have my mind set out to encounter Him. I use the word encounter, more so than meet, because one doesn't simply meet Jesus… it's not like meeting Tom for the first time. It's beyond that, to say it is a life-changing experience would make it sound similar to others who have met the man or woman of their dreams, or did something that changed the way they saw the world. Encountering Jesus is not a life changing experience. *Meeting Jesus is definitely being 'born-again' into a world that is temporary, while at the same time residing in one that is eternal, without physically being there.*

At the time of meeting Him, I was working on Wall Street, making six-figures, and was enjoying the lifestyle of any, early 30-year-old, New York City woman would be expected to enjoy. Clubs, parties, men, traveling around the world, and simply living a marvelous life.

I had friends and family members who called themselves Christians. However, every single person I knew who called themselves Christian were mean, sick, broke, and unhappy. Why would I want to meet someone they said was God, when I was doing better than self-proclaimed Christians? They would get drunk, sleep around, smoke marijuana, promoted that watching pornography was a wonderful past time, and didn't think twice about lying and manipulating people for self-gain. I could not wrap my mind around the notion that they believed in 'a' Jesus Christ, talked about 'a' Jesus Christ, heard messages about Jesus Christ, and yet, used His name in vain, and lived like the one who Jesus Christ supposedly came to defeat.

Along with this, I was often told that "God speaks." "Jesus Christ will guide you if you let Him." "God is real, you need to trust Him with your life!" And a plethora of other things that they believed to be true about Jesus. My response was always, "If God is real, He would talk to me!" Well, while on a plane, He did and He hasn't stopped talking since.

The events that took place on the plane can be read in, *Spiritual Warfare A Fight For Love.* © But the short story is; I had a conversation with Him, encountered the spirit realm, and felt the power of pure love being poured into my body, filling me up from my toes, to the top of my head. I cried during the remaining hours of the flight, from Heathrow, all the way to JFK airport.

While on the plane, and then in the taxi heading home, there were two things that were heavy on my mind. One, I had to find a Bible! *I knew I had one, somewhere in the apartment, but I had no idea where it was. (Sound familiar?)*. And, two, I had reasoned in my mind and heart that I needed to leave my Wall Street job to become a nun, like Mother Teresa. Yes, that's right, a nun. I thought, because I just encountered God, and had revelation that Jesus Christ was/is indeed real, and I had been *saved*, I needed to leave my six-figure job on Wall Street in order to help poor people. This wasn't something that He told me to do, it was something that I 'thought' I had to do because that was all I knew when it came to 'serving God'.

To be clear, it wasn't a 'thought', but an intense yearning to help people. I now know that it was God who gave me that desire. Along with this longing, I also needed to tell everyone I knew that Jesus Christ is real, He is Lord, and He is indeed alive. Note: not, 'was real', but *is* real and alive.

I called my entire family, friends, and so-called-friends, and began to proclaim that God was real, that Jesus is love, and for a lot of them, I had to tell them that they were not saved. I told those who proclaimed to be Christians, that, "they were not saved, that they were not Christians, and they needed to give their lives to Jesus Christ… for real!" You can simply guess how a lot of those conversations went.

Once I arrived to my 1400 sq. ft.[15] apartment in upper Manhattan, I cried for hours. The next day, I saw demonic forces around all of the music and books that I had accumulated over the years. I will share more about this in later chapters, but God did not have to tell me that perverse movies with violence and sex in them didn't please Him. Nor did He have to tell me that I needed to stop partaking in them, I simply knew that I *should not* have them in my home; neither did I *want* them anywhere around me.

---

[15] 130. square meters (EU)/ 40 pyeong (Korea)

As I began to throw everything into big black garbage bags, God spoke and made it clear that I w*as to "Stay on Wall Street!"* He shared that 'He' would tell me when to leave and where to go. As I look back, I now realize that this was the first argument, I had in my heart with God.

There I was, newly saved, having just encountered the pure love of the One who created all things seen and unseen, and I didn't want to do what He said. Remind you of two other people?

The argument wasn't a verbal one, or a debate likened to a disagreement. My heart simply did not want to do what He was telling me to do. How many of us live like that? How many of us, after years of walking with God, refuse to comprehend and apprehend that disobedience is not simply an action or inaction antithetical to what God has said? We must understand that it is a position of our heart caused by rebellion and distrust of God. To be disobedient is to yield to self-will instead of surrendering to God and desiring His will in all things.

One can understand that at the beginning of our walk with Him, we are trying to figure out how everything works. To be honest, how He works. Everyone that I had met shared that when they were born again, it seemed like an automatic desire to want to do what He desired, but yet, were fully aware of the fight that was transpiring between their desire to please Him, and their desire to do what they thought was right. I can attest to this as well. But as we grow in Him and read the Word, we realized that the desire to obey Him is beyond being obedient. It has to do with the way we show love for Him and towards Him. By going where He tells us to go, in order to receive a blessing or be a blessing to someone else...these various acts of obedience is a natural outcome of the love we have for Him and His creation.

When first addressing obedience, after The Fall, we can read how Noah was obedient in building the ark, or Abram was obedient in leaving his father's home. It is actually in Genesis 19, where God refers to obedience.

3 Then Moses went up to God, and the LORD called to him from the mountain and said, "This is what you are to say to the house of Jacob and what you are to tell the people of Israel: 4 'You yourselves have seen what I did to Egypt, and how I carried you on eagles' wings and brought you to myself. 5 *Now if you obey me fully and keep my covenant, then out of all nations you will be my treasured possession. Although the whole earth is mine,* 6 *you will be for me a kingdom of priests and a holy nation.' These are the words you are to speak to the Israelites."* (Genesis 19:3-6).

It is here where we see that God gives us a choice to obey. He uses the word, '*if*' throughout His word to connote that we have a *free will choice* to follow what He has said, or choose to go in a direction that is not His.

We can also refer to Deuteronomy 11:26-28, where God clearly says, '*you have a choice*'. "*See, I am setting before you today a blessing and a curse - the blessing if you obey the commands of the Lord your God that I am giving you today; the curse if you disobey the commands of the Lord your God and turn from the way that I command you today by following other gods, which you have not known.*"

And, for those who want to respond to the above with, "well that was the Old Testament", here we have similar statements in the New Testament.

"If you love me, you will obey what I command...Whoever has my commands, and obeys them he is the one who loves me. He who loves me will be loved by my Father, and I too will love him and show myself to him" (John 14:15, John 14:21).

"Why do you call me, "Lord, Lord, and do not do what I say?" (Luke 6:46)

"Do not merely listen to the word, and so deceive yourselves. Do what it says" (James 1:22).

God has consistently shown that if we obey Him, we will be blessed. If we choose to obey Him, we are showing that we love Him. If we believe Him, then we will do what He says. When we don't obey Him, we must ask, *is it an issue of not believing Him?* Or, is it an issue of not really believing in Him? Whichever the reason, it is up to you to determine, and for you and God to resolve. As for me, I had no clue as to why He was telling me to do something different from what 'I' had already set my mind to do.

The complaint was, why should I have to stay on Wall Street? *Those* people were liars and perverted in every way. From sex, drugs, corruption, profanity, you name it, or better yet, you've seen it all depicted in various movies about the scandalous and corruptible activities of working on Wall Street. I simply resolved that I did not want to continue to work in an environment that grieved me in so many ways.

God showed me later that it wasn't an issue of staying in the environment that I was living in for most of my life. Meaning, I had begun working on Wall Street at the age of 18. I had worked with various companies and understood what it took to move up in the cut-throat environment.

However, during the process of staying on Wall Street and after being moved off of Wall Street, I discovered two reasons as to why God did not plan for me to leave at the time I wanted to depart.

First, He was dealing with my self-righteous attitude of, 'me versus them'. I was saved, devouring the Word, and being loved by God. 'I' did not want to be around, nor thought that I needed to be around people who were just as I was only a few weeks prior.

I did not realize how easy it was for me to see myself as being better than them, and how I had a disdain for those who walked in what I lived in all of my life. There were those who thought they were 'nice' because of the many things they did and did not do. Given such, they, along with myself believed that we were 'good people'. But in reality, no one is good, absolutely no one. The more you think you are good, the more you are in need of the ONLY one who is good, and that is God.

Second, He was preparing a place for me and I did not see it until I was 'there'. He is the only one who knows the timing of the steps that we are to take. Once we surrender our life to Him, He will be in complete and total control of our lives, as it relates to planning and ordering our steps. Some would say, "He is now in complete and total charge!" But in actuality, God does not negate your free will to choose to follow Him. Granted there are some stories that I can share, as well as those that I have heard, where it appears as though He totally over-rode our free will, but those are stories for another time and another book.

However, when we choose Him, it becomes His responsibility to take full and complete care of us in every detail of our lives – including finding the next position, who to marry, where to go and what to do. There isn't one area, or detail that He hasn't already planned out, and the Holy Spirit, the Helper, is assigned to show and guide us into all that we are to do and become.

For most people, at the beginning of their walk, waiting can really be daunting. And for some, (pointing at myself) it could literally feel like torture. But I *now* know, this is how God develops the fruit of patience and faith, along with other things in our personality.

While dealing with staying on Wall Street, and being newly saved, I did not know that I had to have full faith, trust, and belief that God had my life completely in His hands. Over time, I learned that He, in His perfect timing, would reveal the right place and perfect timing for me to transition from where I was, to where He desired for me to be.

While going through the process of staying, and not moving until God directed me, I did not simply sit and complain. I read the Bible every day and asked a lot of questions. I knew that I needed to understand what had happened to me, why was I seeing angels and demons, why was I hearing God, and why was I seeing things on, and around people?

It took seven months from the day I was saved for God to move me to another location. However, I did not realize that it was seven months until years later when I began to write about all that God had walked me through. During the transition, it 'felt' like years. I realized that it felt like years not only because of what was happening in my life, naturally and supernaturally, but I had also told everyone. Some of whom I should not have due to their lack of belief in God. Lack of belief that God speaks and most importantly, and the one that impacted me the most, my family who stated, "Why would God tell you to leave all that money!"

Eventually, God moved me from my six-figure job in Manhattan to a place in Los Angeles, where my income went down substantially from what I was making, and my expenses increased by three times from what they were while I was living in New York City.

I realized then that it wasn't simply me being obedient to Him telling me to stay on Wall Street, but it was now being obedient to moving to a city that I did not know. Yes, I knew of California and had friends who have traveled there, but honestly, I had no desire to visit the land of earthquakes and 'hoooot' weather. In addition, I was going to be making less money, and be away from every family member and friend that I had loved. Even though those factors were prevalent, it was harder to stay than to go. But once I went, I saw the hand of God, and learned His ways of doing things that words would never be able to fully describe. From Him paying my rent, putting gas in my car, angels picking up my car and keeping me from accidents, to God taking me through the process of learning to hear, follow, love and bask in Him loving me back, I would have never developed a deeper love for Him if I had disobeyed.

Whether God tells you to go or to stay, to do something specific, or to sit still, He is the one who knows what is waiting for you with each step you take.

The Red Coat

While waiting to leave New York City, there were a number of situations that I now look back on and laugh. One such situation was associated with a bright red coat that I received from my aunt Jackie.

Jackie had given me a red coat that she thought looked perfect on me. However, I regularly wore black coats that matched my black or dark blue wardrobe that was most appropriate for a Wall Street woman. Nonetheless, when she gave me the coat I happily took it and hung it in the back of my closet thinking that one day, it would eventually grow on me.

One morning as I was preparing to leave for work, I felt as though I needed to take the coat with me. It was a clear feeling of 'take the coat', not 'wear the coat'. But as I was learning to hear and obey, I ignored the feeling as I rushed out my apartment.

As I had previously mentioned, I had a very nice apartment, in upper-Manhattan, but, I lived on the 5th floor of a five-floor walk-up. Once I was downstairs, I had no plans of going back up. However, I made it the 3rd floor 39 before sensing a feeling I had never felt before. The best way   to describe it is when you *KNOW*

YOU SHOULD HAVE DONE something but you didn't, and you were going to get into trouble later because it wasn't done. So, I turned back around, ran back up to the 5th floor and got the coat.

I also had a garbage bag to discard in the dumping area of my building. As I approached the gated garbage area, there was a homeless woman going through the garbage. Given the fact that I lived in a gated community where even the garbage area was gated, I wondered how she was able to enter the locked area. When she saw me, she was startled, but I looked at her as if to say, 'Don't worry'. I dumped my garbage and proceeded to rush off to work.

Once I got about 50 feet away, it was as if someone lovingly slapped me in the back of my head. The coat was for her! We can get so caught up in trying to figure out what God wants us to do while missing what He puts right in front of us.

As I turned around to return to the garbage area, the building superintendent[16] was yelling at the woman, while shooing her away. As I approached them, he looked at me and gave me a big smile and said, "Good Morning." The frightened woman was trying to figure out what to do, in order to pass through all of the garbage bags in order to run away. But in my limited Spanish, I told her to wait, and I gave her the red coat. As I handed her the coat, the building superintendent was clearly annoyed and grumbling. However, the women, with a dingy face, and layers of rags, looked at me and smiled with tears in her eyes. She said in Spanish, the building superintendent translated. "I asked God if He had forgotten about me, and if He hadn't could He give me a red coat."

I cannot explain what happened from that moment for the rest of the day. I know that I had gotten on the train, worked a full day and returned home. But all I can remember was being in total bewilderment as to what was happening to me, and how that could be orchestrated. The fact that He put it on my aunt's heart to give me her red coat, the unction to take it with me, encountering the angry superintendent, and then the homeless lady. I was beginning to learn how God would line

---

[16]A building superintendent or building supervisor (often shortened to super) is a manager responsible for repair and maintenance in a residential building. They are the first point of contact for residents of the building.

up things and people, at an appointed time in order for His will to be done.

Even as I recall that moment as well as the hundreds of others, and I am sure as you read this you can think of some of your own, my question is, why do we, take even seconds to 'doubt' and wonder if we are where we are supposed to be, or doing what we are supposed to be doing?"

Why do we second-guess if we hear God, or whether God spoke in order to direct us to do something...which a lot of times makes no sense to us?

There were a number of assignments that God had given me during those first few months of being saved, from leaving work early, driving to another state in order to see a well-known evangelist, to going to a certain place and waiting to give someone a prophetic word, a specific amount of money, or a word of encouragement. It was clear to me that He was teaching me to not only hear His voice but to trust that as I went to where He guided, it would be a blessing for someone else.

I realized that obedience to His voice was not simply for me to benefit, but most of the time, it is to bring or be the answer to prayer for someone else. The excitement and the love I feel to be used by Him, *to bring joy to those who need it, is one of the blessings of being obedient.*

Most Christians think that being transformed into the image of Christ requires, simply, renewing our minds with the reading of the Word. We focus on Romans 12:2, "Do not conform to the pattern of this world, but be transformed by the renewing of your mind. Then you will be able to test and approve what God's will is-his good, pleasing and perfect will." However, we can possibly miss the main point, *obeying God is the active process of being transformed.* Following His lead is walking according to His will, in thoughts, words, and deeds. It is then, and only then we know that we are in His good, pleasing and perfect will.

When we think about Jesus obeying His father, He declares, in John 6:38, "For I have come down from heaven, not to do my own will but the will of him who sent me." (Emphasis mine). Jesus provided a magnificent example of what obedience looks like when He went to the cross, and each thing He did prior to the cross. He humbled himself and forfeited being with our Father in order to manifest himself completely as man. Since God did this for us, why is it so hard for some to humble themselves, in order to die to what they want to do, and hold on to each directive He presents?

Jesus' obedience offers hope, peace, joy and everlasting life to all who would receive him. And, had He not humbled himself and became obedient unto the death on the cross, we would remain in our sins and hope. You can apply this to yourself as well. When you do not go where God leads you, or do what He desires for you to do, you will be holding back a measure of peace, joy, hope, and other blessings from those who God desires to bless. Jesus chose to obey, why can't you? He is living in you and has empowered you to do so. Therefore the question remains, Do you have the One you say you have and if so, why is obeying Him so difficult?"

Seeking Wisdom of Man and Institutions

I love school! I love everything about the academic process. I even appreciate writing papers and taking tests. However, the thing that I enjoy most is the interaction between fellow students that is required in order to develop reasoning and other critical thinking skills. Given that God knows that I love school, He also knew that school would be one of the things I would run to after being saved.

I knew about convents, which is where people go to become or live as nuns. I also knew about Christian universities, but I had no idea that seminaries existed. I didn't know that there were degrees that you could earn in various biblical studies and when I found out, my heart leaped at the chance of being able to attend.

After God moved me to California, I found out that my main office was located only five minutes from a well-known seminary. I was excited and elated believing that this was something God wanted me to do… because "I" wanted to do it.

After filling out all of the forms and submitting the required information, I was called in for an interview. During the interview, I excitedly shared with the admissions counselor, how I got saved and ended up in California. Half way through my testimony, she interrupted me, excused herself and returned with someone else. She told me to start my story over from the beginning. Needless to say, I was accepted and was informed as to when I should arrive for orientation.

During that time, I was already enrolled in a Ph.D. program for Organizational Behavior specializing in Information Technology Management. I had also started an online program with Oxford University in order to earn a Diploma in Computer Science, and attending the Los Angeles Institute of Leadership and Ministry in order to take courses on Christianity and Leadership. All of this while working a full-time job. Nevertheless, I was excited to be able to study the Word with other people who loved God so much that they would spend two to four years studying about Him.

The first day of orientation came, and I was ready. I felt like it was my first day of kindergarten and the anticipation was overwhelming. After arriving at the school and signing in, I found an empty seat at a table that had a few men and women. As they all began to introduce themselves, most of them had been in some form of ministry for a number of years. They had shared about their marital status, and the number of children they had. As I listened, I got more and more excited because I realized that I would be able to befriend Christians who were well seasoned in walking with the Lord because I was only saved for nine months at the time.

Before we could finish introducing ourselves, a representative of the school began to pray, and then explain the vision of the school as well as the various programs offered by the school. As he shared all of the amazing things that the school had accomplished with preparing students for their future in ministry, which could be as pastors, missionaries, or teachers, I was listening for him to share as it relates to those who were not going to be pastors, missionaries, evangelist or teachers. My mind started to run with what my research was going to be on, and that was ministering to wealthy business people and politicians. I did not know at the time that this type of ministry was called, 'Marketplace' ministry.

As I was writing my notes on how I was going to formulate a research paper that would be required at the end of the two-year program, JESUS... yes, Jesus came over to our table, stood right next to me and it was as if He was saying, with arms crossed… not angrily or intimidating, but with a loving and tender voice, "***Daddy did not tell you to do this!***" I quickly packed up my things, while my new acquaintances looked on confused, and walked out knowing that I was not going to attend seminary anytime soon.

As I drove home crying, wanting to know why, God clearly said, ***I will show you, I will teach you, and I will be with you.***

From that day on, I knew that as I walked with Him, He would guide my steps, help me to get up after falling, and continue to ensure that I was where I was meant to be, doing what I was supposed to be doing, and if I had missed it, gently put me back on track.

"The Lord directs the steps of the godly. He delights in every detail of their lives. Though they stumble, they will never fall, for the Lord holds them by the hand." (Psalm 37:23-24).

He Provides Oil

There were countless times where God provided exactly what was needed in order for me to obey what He was guiding me to do. It *is* a training that everyone I have encountered goes through where we all have come to realize that He does not only train us as it relates to hearing Him, but He is training us to trust Him completely to provide all that we need.

After returning from my 2nd trip to Israel, with the 3rd one to be within a few more weeks, I was prepared to relax at home and recoup from the month-long whirlwind excursion to Martha's Vineyard and Israel with friends. However, God instructed me to drive to Knoxville, Tennessee.

I wasn't sure why He wanted me to go, but after some research, I saw that there was a conference scheduled to be held by a ministry that is based there, the same weekend God told me to go. The conferences had a number of pastors and ministers scheduled to speak who I had never heard of, but there was one that I had heard, speak at my home church. So, I registered for the four-day conference.

A week before the conference, in an open vision, I saw two large red containers and the number five on the front of them. I felt like I should buy them.

When I researched, red 5-gallon containers, I discovered that they were gasoline containers. I must admit that I let a number of days go by. But by the following Friday, the day before the conference, while returning home from church, I practically felt like God was going to give me a spanking if I did not get those containers. To be clear, God does not spank us. However, for those of you who knew you did something wrong while growing up, and you knew that you would be in trouble once your parents returned home, that feeling of waiting for one of them to walk through the door, was the feeling I had when I was being 'disobedient' with getting the two containers.

Allow me to explain it another way. It is that feeling that I am sure you all have had in the pit of your stomach when you knew that you were supposed to do something and you did not do it. The best way to describe it is when you say to yourself that you 'should do something', like take your umbrella, even though the weatherman called for sunny skies, but you leave the house without it. Throughout the day, it keeps nagging you in the back of your mind that you should have brought the umbrella. Your manager asks you to stay late, and when you leave out of the office, it is pouring rain.

Well, it's a feeling similar to that, but when it comes to Holy Spirit and interacting with Him, it's like a friend who is with you all the time and it is as though they are giving you that look that says, "Yes, I am your friend, I love you dearly, but you know what you are supposed to do, or should be doing, so get to it".

So, I went to the only place that I knew would be open at 11:30 pm and would have the containers. I purchased the two containers and went to a gas station near my home and filled both containers with gasoline.

While doing so, a man who was purchasing gas asked me why was I filling up containers? I smiled and said "God told me to do so." Of course he looked at me like I was crazy but I simply smiled and kept filling my containers.

The next day, I placed both containers in the trunk of my car and left for Tennessee. As I drove past the same gas station, and every other station within six miles of my house there were large **NO GAS** signs posted, or the lights were off at the stations. I turned on the radio to see if I could find out what was going on. Low and behold, there was a gas shortage.

According to news reports, hurricane-related disruptions in the supply of fuel from Gulf Coast refineries led stations in Atlanta and elsewhere to run out of gas. People spent days searching for gas in the Atlanta area and other parts of the Southeast. The Southeast experienced a hurricane-triggered gas shortage that threw the region's gas stations into chaos. All but two of the Gulf Coast refineries were not affected by Hurricanes Ike and Gustav.

The refineries along the Gulf of Mexico that supplied the majority of the Southeast's gas lines reaching Virginia in the East and as far north as Chicago suffered the most. A bulk of the Northeast received oil through barge shipments, and the West Coast was supplied mainly from refineries and pipelines in California, so hurricanes tend to spur gasoline shortages in the Southeast. Being that the hurricanes caused widespread power outages on the Gulf Coast, which forced refineries to shut down, many people went for days without being able to purchase gas.

I could not believe my ears. As I turned onto the highway, I cried and praised the Lord at how He provided gas. I was able to drive to Knoxville TN, and return home knowing that God provided, yet again.

While reflecting on the above story, the account of the virgins and the oil comes to mind. You should take some time and study this parable so that you can ask yourself if your lamp is full and ready for His return.

The Parable of the Wise and Foolish Virgins

"Then the kingdom of heaven shall be likened to ten virgins who took their lamps and went out to meet the bridegroom. 2 Now five of them were wise, and five were foolish. 3 Those who were foolish took their lamps and took no oil with them, 4 but the wise took oil in their vessels with their lamps. 5 But while the bridegroom was delayed, they all slumbered and slept. 6 "And at midnight a cry was heard: 'Behold, the bridegroom is coming; go out to meet him!'

7 Then all those virgins arose and trimmed their lamps. 8 And the foolish said to the wise, 'Give us some of your oil, for our lamps are going out.' 9 But the wise answered, saying, 'No, lest there should not be enough for us and you; but go rather to those who sell, and buy for yourselves.' 10 And while they went to buy, the bridegroom came, and those who were ready went in with him to the wedding; and the door was shut. 11 "Afterward the other virgins came also, saying, 'Lord, Lord, open to us!' 12 But he answered and said, 'Assuredly, I say to you, I do not know you.' 13 "Watch therefore, for you know neither the day nor the hour in which the Son of Man is coming. (Matthew 25:1-13)

We should remember that the above parable was spoken by Jesus in response to the disciples' request to know what sign would signal our Lord's coming and the end of the age. (Matthew 24:3). Jesus spoke to them about the last days. He made it clear that the end would not come immediately, but only after considerable time and troubles (Matthew 24:4-31). Jesus issued various warnings (Matthew 24:4-5, 10-11, 23-28), because during these troubled times there would be many interlopers, who would seek to turn man's attention and affections away from Jesus, the true Messiah.[17]

There are a number of commentaries that give an explanation of the parable, but one thing is clear, those with oil in their lamps went with the bridegroom and there were those without oil, who were not allowed to go.

Some have said that the five virgins who had the oil represent the truly born again who are looking with eagerness to the coming of Christ. They have saving faith and have determined that, whatever occurs when Jesus returns, they will be looking with eagerness and focused on the one who truly has their heart.

However, the five virgins without the oil represent false believers who enjoy the benefits of the Christian community without truly loving

---

[17]26. The Ten Virgins: What It Means to Be Ready (Matthew 25:1-13) April 27th 2005. https://Bible.org/seriespage/26-ten-virgins-what-it-means-be-ready-matthew-251-13

Christ. They are more concerned about the association with the title of 'Christian' than longing to see the bridegroom. Their hope is that their association with true believers ("give us some of your oil" of verse 8) will bring them into the kingdom at the end.

I realized that it is clear throughout scriptures that an individual's faith in Jesus cannot save another. The "Lord, Lord" and "I do not know you" of verses 11 and 12 fit very well with Jesus' condemnation of the false believers of Matthew 7:21-23, "Not everyone who says to Me, 'Lord, Lord,' will enter the kingdom of heaven, but he who does the will of My Father who is in heaven will enter. Many will say to Me on that day, 'Lord, Lord, did we not prophesy in Your name, and in Your name cast out demons, and in Your name perform many miracles?' And then I will declare to them, 'I never knew you; depart from Me, you who practice lawlessness.'"

Walking in obedience doesn't just ensure that we are in God's perfect will as it relates to doing what He requires of us. It keeps the oil we have in our lamps full and ready to be received by Him.

While reflecting on the above, I 'just' googled, *5-gallon red container* and discovered that the containers I picked were called *Scepter!!!!*

A scepter, also known as a rod or mace used by a sovereign as a symbol of royal authority. The kingship of Yahweh is spoken of as a scepter (Psalms 45:6 (Hebrew verse 7) quoted in Hebrews 1:8). The manner of using the scepter by an oriental monarch is suggested in the act of Ahasuerus, who holds it out to Esther as a mark of favor. (Esther 5:2).

It never ceases to amaze me how when we delve in deeper into what God is revealing, He surprises us with information on how every step we take in obedience to Him, the meaning of what appears to be irrelevant, is deeper than we could ever imagine.

What is also interesting is that the purpose of the conference was to revive, refresh, heal, equip and release the body of Christ with a fresh impartation of the presence and power of God. The organizing ministry was led by a pastor who believed that the same presence and power that Jesus manifested in His single human body, He will also manifest through His corporate body, the Church. The organizer was passionate about training believers so that they can be equipped to do the work of ministry, and wanted all of those in attendance to fully understand that we are not only the Bride of Christ, but also a royal priesthood.

After arriving at the hotel and parking my car, I began to become fearful of the fact that I had 10 gallons of gas in the trunk of my car. I wasn't sure if it would be safe given the fact that we all know that gasoline is a flammable liquid and should be stored at room temperature, away from potential heat sources such as the sun, hot water heaters, space heater or a furnace, and at least 50 feet away from ignition sources, such as pilot lights. And, given that gasoline vapors are heavier than air and can travel along the floor to ignite, I wasn't sure where I should park. Thankfully there was a custodian worker in the garage, and I was able to ask him. He told me that the gas should be fine and assured me there shouldn't be any explosion. Even though he informed me of such, I prayed accordingly.

The first evening in Knoxville, I sat in the meeting waiting for it to start. A husband and wife couple sat right next to me, and after introductions, the husband inquired as to the name of the church I attended. I proudly told him and the couple's mouths dropped wide open and proceeded to tell me that they were Assistant Pastors at the same church some years back. As-a-matter-of-fact, the husband helped build the sanctuary that is currently being used.

From staying on Wall Street to giving a homeless woman a coat. To staying in one university, while dropping out of another, (I had started Oxford as well, but God woke me up one night and told me to drop out), God is the one who always knows what we should do and when it should be done.

He not only gives us the directive, but He makes sure that He provides the provision and resources needed to accomplish what He desires.

I often think of the man who I met at the gas station. I wonder if he still talks about the woman he met who was filling up the containers, the one that told him that God told her to do so. I wonder if he went on to research/question/determine if God was real... and if so, I pray that he discovered that Jesus is indeed alive.

Stumbling & Getting Back Up

Saul Spares King Agag

15 Samuel also said to Saul, "The Lord sent me to anoint you king over His people, over Israel. Now therefore, heed the voice of the words of the Lord. 2 Thus says the Lord of hosts: 'I will punish Amalek for what he did to Israel, how he ambushed him on the way when he came up from Egypt. 3 Now go and attack Amalek, and utterly destroy all that they have, and do not spare them. But kill both man and woman, infant and nursing child, ox and sheep, camel and donkey.'" 4 So Saul gathered the people together and numbered them in Telaim, two hundred thousand foot soldiers and ten thousand men of Judah. 5 And Saul came to a city of Amalek, and lay in wait in the valley. 6 Then Saul said to the Kenites, "Go, depart, get down from among the Amalekites, lest I destroy you with them. For you showed kindness to all the children of Israel when they came up out of Egypt." So the Kenites departed from among the Amalekites. 7 And Saul attacked the Amalekites, from Havilah all the way to Shur, which is east of Egypt. 8 He also took Agag king of the Amalekites alive, and utterly destroyed all the people with the edge of the sword. 9 But Saul and the people spared Agag and the best of the sheep, the oxen, the fatlings, the lambs, and all that was good, and were unwilling to utterly destroy them. But everything despised and worthless, that they utterly destroyed.

Saul Rejected as King

10 Now the word of the Lord came to Samuel, saying, 11 "I greatly regret that I have set up Saul as king, for he has turned back from following Me, and has not performed My commandments." And it grieved Samuel, and he cried out to the Lord all night. 12 So when Samuel rose early in the morning to meet Saul, it was told Samuel, saying, "Saul went to Carmel, and indeed, he set up a monument for himself; and he has gone on around, passed by, and gone down to Gilgal." 13 Then Samuel went to Saul, and Saul said to him, "Blessed are you of the Lord! I have performed the commandment of the Lord." 14 But Samuel said, "What then is this bleating of the sheep in my ears, and the lowing of the oxen which I hear?" 15 And Saul said, "They have brought them from the Amalekites; for the people spared the best of the sheep and the oxen, to sacrifice to the Lord your God; and the rest we have utterly destroyed." 16 Then Samuel said to Saul, "Be quiet! And I will tell you what the Lord said to me last night." And he said to him, "Speak on."

17 So Samuel said, "When you were little in your own eyes, were you not head of the tribes of Israel? And did not the Lord anoint you king over Israel? 18 Now

the Lord sent you on a mission, and said, 'Go, and utterly destroy the sinners, the Amalekites, and fight against them until they are consumed.' 19 Why then did you not obey the voice of the Lord? Why did you swoop down on the spoil, and do evil in the sight of the Lord?"

20 And Saul said to Samuel, "But I have obeyed the voice of the Lord, and gone on the mission on which the Lord sent me, and brought back Agag king of Amalek; I have utterly destroyed the Amalekites. 21 But the people took of the plunder, sheep and oxen, the best of the things which should have been utterly destroyed, to sacrifice to the Lord your God in Gilgal."

22 So Samuel said: "Has the Lord as great delight in burnt offerings and sacrifices, As in obeying the voice of the Lord? Behold, to obey is better than sacrifice, And to heed than the fat of rams. 23 For rebellion is as the sin of witchcraft, And stubbornness is as iniquity and idolatry.

Because you have rejected the word of the Lord, He also has rejected you from being king."

24 Then Saul said to Samuel, "I have sinned, for I have transgressed the commandment of the Lord and your words, **because I feared the people and obeyed their voice**. 25 Now therefore, please pardon my sin, and return with me, that I may worship the Lord."

26 But Samuel said to Saul, "I will not return with you, for you have rejected the word of the Lord, and the Lord has rejected you from being king over Israel." 27 And as Samuel turned around to go away, Saul seized the edge of his robe, and it tore. 28 So Samuel said to him, "The Lord has torn the kingdom of Israel from you today, and has given it to a neighbor of yours, who is better than you. 29 And also the Strength of Israel will not lie nor relent. For He is not a man that He should relent." 30 Then he said, "I have sinned; yet honor me now, please, before the elders of my people and before Israel, and return with me, that I may worship the Lord your God." 31 So Samuel turned back after Saul, and Saul worshiped the Lord. 32 Then Samuel said, "Bring Agag king of the Amalekites here to me." So Agag came to him cautiously. And Agag said, "Surely the bitterness of death is past." 33 But Samuel said, "As your sword has made women childless, so shall your mother be childless among women." And Samuel hacked Agag in pieces before the Lord in Gilgal. 34 Then Samuel went to Ramah, and Saul went up to his house at Gibeah of Saul. 35 And Samuel went no more to see Saul until the day of his

death. Nevertheless Samuel mourned for Saul, and the Lord regretted that He had made Saul king over Israel.[18] (1 Samuel 15: 15-35 New King James Version)

Matthew 10:28"Do not fear those who kill the body but are unable to kill the soul; but rather fear Him who is able to destroy both soul and body in hell.

Have you ever wondered why Saul disobeyed God when God told him what to do? How it is that one can encounter God and yet still be afraid of people's opinions? How does one, know without a shadow of doubt that God is alive and real, and yet still struggle with the 'fear of man' and believe that it is better to appease man than to obey and follow the instructions of the one who is the giver of life? I am sure, as you read this, you can think of a number of times that you allowed the fear of man to either delay or prevent you from doing or saying something that God required of you. But looking at Saul, we can see how appeasing man can be our downfall.

First, Saul was chosen by God to be the first king for the Israelites. Saul knew that God had chosen him, and God chose him by using Samuel to do so. Subsequently, Samuel gave Saul specific instructions to follow, and yet, Saul yielded to the desires of the people he was leading. What is interesting with this part of the story is that, they followed Saul into battle, but yet, Saul followed them when it came to seizing plunder from the battle. It was evident, at this point that Saul wasn't the leader, but a follower of the desires of those he wanted to please. We have to learn that we cannot please man and God, especially when we have to choose between the two. In actuality, there should never be a *choice*, when you are truly saved and free to love Jesus.

The most poignant issue about this story was Saul's double-mindedness. He knew what he was supposed to do and chose not to do it. He then acted like he obeyed when knew he did not. He knew that he did not follow God's instructions, but yet, when Samuel arrived and confronted him, he not only made excuses for not doing what God

---

[18]Scripture taken from the New King James Version®. Copyright © 1982 by Thomas Nelson. Used by permission. All rights reserved.

instructed him to do, he acted like he did do what was supposed to have been done.

Disobedience opens the door wide for confusions and double-mindedness. And the Bible says, a double minded man is unstable in all his ways and shall receive nothing from the Lord. (James 1:8)

What is a double minded person? They are consistently confused in their mind; restless in their thoughts, unsettled in their designs and intentions, inconstant in their petitions, uncertain in their notions and opinion of things, and very variable in their actions. They are always changing, and never at a point, but at a continual uncertainty, both in their thinking and doing. They never continue long in an opinion, or in a practice, but are always shifting and moving. The thing to remember, they morph into what the people around them desire.

I remember hearing a pastor once say, "There is nothing scarier than a double minded, people pleasing person who will morph into the needs of those around them!"

This does not mean that you don't find yourself at times trying to make a decision as to what to do, or trying to determine which direction God wants you to go. A double minded person is someone who, as described above, is at peace one day, and then the next day, they are emotionally distraught. Angry one day, and then a few days later, act as though nothing happened. Today, people may call this type of behavior a number of things, but in reality, the Bible says that God will keep a man in perfect peace whose mind is stayed on Him. A double minded person's mind is *not* on God.

"The steadfast of mind you will keep in perfect peace, because he trusts in you. 4 "Trust in the LORD forever, For in GOD the LORD, we have an everlasting Rock. (Isaiah, 26:3)

When it comes to obeying God, one cannot expect a double minded person to follow the leading of the Holy Spirit. Why? Because a double-minded person is restless and confused in his thoughts, his actions, and his behavior. Such a person is always in conflict with himself. One torn by such inner conflict can never lean with confidence on God and His gracious promises. But when we look deeper, it's more than having confidence in God, it's an issue of, "do they believe in God?"

I know some may think that asking that question is punitive, but the reality is,

...if someone proclaims to believe in God, and has made Jesus Christ his/her Lord and Savior, how is it possible for the person to live a life, where they are constantly wavering between doing what 'people' want him/her to do, versus what God wants?

Saul believed in God, but Saul clearly did not 'make' God his god. The days that Saul spent waiting for Samuel to return were clearly being used to teach Saul patience and dependence upon God. When he did not wait, he showed a variety of weaknesses that made him unfit as a king, including impatience and self-reliance. His offering showed that he did not want to work together with Samuel or obey God, but rather took control of the situation himself. The king was to follow the Lord's commands, yet Saul felt that he could do as he pleased and thus made a foolish mistake. Another indirect reason why Saul's action was wrong is that Saul was not a priest or Levite. Therefore, he could not legally offer a burnt offering or peace offering. Saul was of the tribe of Benjamin and was not to do the work of a priest. However, the biblical text notes that the direct reason why Saul's sacrifice was sinful was that Saul disobeyed Samuel's command. Samuel was a prophet and person of authority, and the word of the Lord was spoken through him to Saul.

Ask yourself, have you truly made God the Lord of your life? If you answered "yes", then you should be able to say that you are at peace in your mind and heart. However, if you said, "yes", and yet you have no peace, then you need to determine if that "yes" is indeed true.

Wall Street to the Desert

One of the things that I had prided myself on, was the fact that I was always the youngest, only African-American woman, and the only, *everything* else in the rooms that I walked into while working on Wall Street.

My first position on Wall Street was working for a legal firm that provided services for unions in NYC. However, by the time I was saved, I was working for an international investment firm where I was the Assistant Vice President managing assets worth billions of dollars.

I had a wonderful apartment in upper Manhattan, where the rent was rent-stabilized.[19] My rent was only 6% of my monthly income, where it is advised that your rent should not be more than 30% of your monthly income. Needless to say, my apartment was both inexpensive and fabulous. I lived less than a five-minute walk to the subway, and the subway station that I needed to get to for work, was under my office building. During the winter, I did not need to be outside often, and during the summer, I could easily take a nice walk to wherever I wanted

---

[19]Rent stabilization sets maximum rates for annual rent increases and, as with rent control, entitles tenants to receive required services from their landlords and have their leases renewed. The rent guidelines board meets every year to determine how much the landlord can set future rents on the lease.

to go. In additional, if I worked past 10:00 pm, which I did most nights, the company provided private car service to take me home.

If everything was so perfect, a job that would allow me to pay off my six-figure student loans within two years, versus 30, why would God tell me to move to California?

I gave my life to the Lord in mid-July, but by the end of July, He had said that He was moving me to California. So, what did this naive, newly saved woman do? Tell everybody I knew. I learned later that telling everyone, everything that God is guiding you to do is not smart.

According to my family and a number of friends, they thought that I was crazy because, *"Why would God have you give up a six-figure job, leave a rent-stabilized apartment, and have you move to California when you have never been there?"* I felt not only confused as to how to answer their questions because they did not believe that God spoke or believe in God at all, it was one of the many times where I had to not only trust God at His word, but fight not to put His directives above those who have loved me my entire life. But God and His goodness, would show me little signs of assurance in that I was hearing Him and that He was indeed moving me out of New York City to a land I did not know.

I remember going out to get lunch at a deli across the street from my office building. I rarely, if ever ventured into this particular deli because of the crowds, but on that particular day I did. While waiting in line to pay for my food, the person in front of me pulled out his wallet and there it was a California driver's license. I almost dropped to the floor, but kept it together and just smiled profusely as I waited in line to pay for my order.

As I shared earlier, immediately, after getting saved, I wanted to stop working on Wall Street, but God told me that I would continue working on Wall Street until He said so. 'In the waiting'...I prayed, as well as began to look for a position in California. I did not know where I needed to be, nor did I know anything about California other than, it is three hours behind New York, and there are earthquakes. That's it. Oh, and of course, Hollywood.

At the time, the process of God getting me to California felt like a long and tiresome one, but it was all within a matter of weeks of Him speaking and me landing a job in California. When I first started writing this, I had noted that it was a few months, but in actuality, from mid-July to mid-August, I had got the directive from God and a new position.

Before moving on with the testimony, I have to share something that happened. A few months prior to being saved, my company had a Career Mapping workshop for the analyst in order for them to do some career planning. During the middle of the day, I went to check in on them to see how they were doing and I walked in during the time when the Corporate Trainer was asking them to write down their 'dream job'.

As I sat and listened, I got a piece of tattered scrap paper and wrote down my dream job which was to work within the compliance area of a financial firm where I was responsible for making sure that all of the legal and federal regulations that they had to adhere to were followed accordingly. I did not want to be an auditor, but something similar to a Compliance Officer. I just scribbled it down and left the training room.

As I began to search for jobs in California, there was one position that stood out. It was for an Operational Risk Officer within the Secondary Markets division that would be responsible for managing various compliance related issues for a multi-billion dollar portfolio. I sent off my resume and didn't think anything else about it. Until a week later when I received a call to schedule a phone interview.

The person that I spoke to was head of Human Resources for the Secondary Markets group at the bank. I was informed, that the new Senior Vice President (SVP) was creating a position in order to ensure that everything he was responsible for was managed ethically and legally. There is a reason I am sharing all the details...keep reading.

During the interview, Mr. White asked me a number of questions. I thought I knew the answers to three of the questions, but found out later that two of those three answers were wrong. My response to the other seven questions were, "I have no idea!"

After the interview, I simply knew that I did not get the job. However, 15 minutes later, I received another call from the HR person stating that Mr. White wanted to fly me to Pasadena for an on-site interview. I couldn't believe it. This was only the beginning of God supernaturally doing everything required to move me from NYC to California.

First, the flight. The company booked my flight, reserved my car, and booked my hotel accommodations. Upon reaching the airport, I went to the kiosk to check in and it asked if I wanted an upgrade. For those of you who fly often know that last minute 1st class upgrades can range from $500-$1000. But the screen read, $25. I thought surely this was a mistake, and it meant $250. So, I re-entered my information and the screen read $25 again. I called one of the attendants over and told them that the machine was reading $25. One woman said, "Oh this is clearly a mistake, the upgrades are $XXX (I don't remember the number), I did not hear the rest because I stopped her and said, "Ohhhh noooo this is God and I am taking this." The other attended said out loud "Amen" and helped me purchase my 1st first class ticket.

Once I reached Burbank airport, I had already been in a state of bliss from the 1st class service from God.

As I reached the counter, the attendant was surprised to see me smiling so profusely due to the fact that everyone else appeared to be frustrated or angry due to delayed flights and a host of other issues that can occur at an airport.

She asked me why I was so happy. I told her about Jesus and how He told me to move to California, upgraded my ticket, and put me in contact with someone who I used to work with, but had not seen in almost eight years. She just smiled while entering the 'rental car' details into her computer. She looked up at me and with a big smile said, "Well, let's add to your day, I have changed your car from the economy that the company reserved to a full-size Mustang GT convertible!" I said, "Oh no, please don't do that, I don't want to take advantage of the fact that they are paying for the car." She said, "And given your response, it makes me all the more want to give you the car. I haven't charged them anything, consider this a free upgrade on me." And, you know what I did next? Cried like a baby and blessed the woman profusely.

I had mentioned being in contact with someone I had not seen in almost eight years. Well, I did say that the details do matter indeed. While cleaning out an old email account's inbox that I rarely ever used because I had already established a new email account, I came across an email from a former co-worker who I had worked with at a legal firm. The email was just a quick hello and an update of her email address. The thing that made me actually scream out loud was the fact that she was located in the Los Angeles/Burbank area, which is where I was headed.

I couldn't believe it. The fact that I 'just happened' to be cleaning out my inbox, and 'just happened' to see her name as I was deleting literally thousands of pieces of junk mail was God showing me that I was on track. I reached out to her and sure enough she didn't live too far from where I was going to be. It was simply God letting me know that He has prepared a place for me.

During the interview process, I was seen by various Senior Vice Presidents and it was everything you think it would be as it relates to being interviewed by men who are wealthy. In the end, I got the position and the position in itself is another book. But the point of all of this was, in obeying His leading and everything He was saying, there I was in Southern California where my income went down by 3x what I was making in NYC and my expenses went 'up' 3x when comparing my financial obligations in NYC to what they were going to be in California. Everyone was asking, "How was this God, how could this have been Him?"

Well, here is the thing, being obedient to God isn't always about going up in income, or going up in status as it relates to 'man' and the 'world'! It is about going up in your relationship with Him where you know you hear Him and trust that He is taking you where you need to be. But more importantly becoming exactly who He would have you to become.

Did I cry when I realized that God had me resigning from my six figure salary job, a job that I had worked so hard for? Did I cry when I realized that I would be leaving a place that I called home all of my life? Did I 'wonder', not worry about what He was doing and why He was doing it? The answer is a resounding, 'YES'. But there was one thing that kept me saying 'Yes' to Him...I loved Him and I knew He loved me.

Benny Hinn: The Indian Man

Once I arrived in California, I was given temporary corporate accommodations. I had a one bedroom apartment that had two televisions. One was in the living room, and the other was in the bedroom. I had already stopped watching television, due to the spiritual issues I was encountering while they were on. All of which can be read in *I am Not Crazy, I Know What I See.*© I was in the kitchen one day and I felt like the Lord was guiding me to turn on the television. One thing that I had discovered was that, unlike the other experiences where I had time to do what He said, this particular time was as if I needed to turn on the television immediately. I dried my hands and turned on the television.

It came on to what looked like an Indian man in a white suit singing "Hallelujah". The thought "that's the devil" came into my mind. So, I turned the television off immediately. I went back to the kitchen to finish cooking and I prayed, asking God why He had me turn on the television.

The next day while in my bedroom, I was lying in bed and the feeling of, 'turn on the television' came over me. As I picked up the remote, I first prayed and then turned on the television. There he was again, the Indian looking man with the white suit. He was in what I found out was called a crusade in India, and I saw people falling to the floor without the man touching them. I saw people screaming and looking like they were in pain and crying. I immediately turned the television off and began to pray again.

As I arrived to work in order to continue with the week-long orientation, I met a woman, Lauren, whose parents were ministers. I had not shared with her what was happening in the apartment because at that point in my walk with the Lord, not even a full year, I had already realized that a number of people thought that I was crazy.

As Lauren and I spent more time together, I began to share with her my salvation story and all of the things that were happening, along with what I was seeing. She began to tell me that what I was sharing was normal and began to tell me about other well-known ministers who had similar stories.

A few weeks later, Lauren invited me to a crusade with a man by the name of Benny Hinn. I had never heard of him nor did I think to research him. After my encounter with Jesus at the seminary, I was not lead to research other ministers, missionaries, or pastors. I trusted that God would tell me what I needed and guide me to those who I needed to be around.

I joined her, along with her mother and father, and made the trip to Long Beach. During the drive, she had me share with her parents some of the various stories I had shared with her. They laughed at a number of them and were amazed that I could talk as fast as I did. I was just so happy to be able to share what was going on in my life with other people who understood what was happening.

Once we reached the arena, we had nosebleed seats.[20] As we waited for the event to begin, I remember hearing various conversations around me that consisted of people saying that Benny Hinn was a false prophet. It was all negative and I wondered, what have 'I' gotten myself into. At the same time, I began to feel the fear of the Lord. Feeling the fear of

---

[20]In the United States and Canada, the nosebleed section (or nosebleed seats) are those seats of a public arena, usually an athletic stadium or gymnasium that are highest and, usually, farthest from the desired activity.

the Lord is different for everyone, so I won't go into sharing the details here, but I simply began to pray and wait.

As the music began and people started walking out on the stage, the music started and people started to sing. At this time of writing, I cannot remember how long the singing went on, but one thing I will never forget... *the angels of fire that flooded the stage in an army like formation.* I asked Lauren if she could see what I was seeing and she said no.

As the angels came out on stage, it was as if there were thousands of them, and then suddenly, out walked the Indian man in the white suit that I had seen twice on my televisions in the apartment... it was Benny Hinn.

As soon as I realized that it was 'The Indian man in the white suit' I began to pray that God had mercy first on me for believing the lie that I entertained while in my apartment. But, I must share, after I asked God to forgive me, I was led to intercede for the people that were surrounding me who were bad mouthing this man I knew nothing about. I shared with Lauren what was going on and proceeded to pray for the people as well as the man on stage. It was at that point in time that God began to teach me that we do not, and should never join in with gossiping, and speaking negatively about anyone in ministry.

We are to ensure that when men and women who are used by God, act in a way that isn't God, we are to pray accordingly as led by God and not by those who gossip behind closed doors, or even out in the open for all to hear. It is God who will in the end decree a final judgment on the person and the ministry. And, if we believe that all things work together for the good of those who love God and are called according to His purpose, then we need to pray for God's perfect will in the lives of those who may not do things the way, 'you' or 'I' think they should be done.

After the meeting, I was on cloud nine. I had never seen so many people healed, and set free. I thought, now this is the book of Acts, the Bible is indeed alive.

I had mentioned that I was happy to be around people who would listen to my many testimonies, without thinking that I was crazy. There were a number of people, pastors, churches, family members, and friends that I would share how God would tell me to give, or go, or do something specific. And all His directives always involved helping someone or giving someone a prophetic word. But I was told, that "God does not speak", "God does not speak to women", "God only speaks through His Word", "God does not heal", and a host of other things that not only made me read the Bible more, but also instilled in me a tenacity to 'Believe God' and those who walk according to what the Bible says.

For example, I told a Reverend that I had been seeing angels and demons around people. And, as I sat in his office, I could see demons walking up and down the hallway of the church, and in his office. He, of course got angry, but I began to explain why they were there, specifically in his office. As I shared with him what he was secretly doing, he of course became even angrier and proceeded to ask me to leave his office.

I was not rebuking him because of the sin he was in, but simply letting him know why the demons were in his office. He was shocked that I knew the details of some very personal matters. But I was more interested in figuring out how I could feel the love that I felt God had for this man, even though he was walking in sin.

It was at this time that I started searching out scriptures, and praying to God about loving those who clearly either didn't love Him, or are pretending to love Him. I wanted to understand the love of Christ and how, even in people's sin, Christ has His arm opened wide open saying, come to me and I will give you rest.

After returning home from the Benny Hinn event, I started to search out his videos online and read articles about him. Well, after about a ½ hour of research, God said "*I will **tell you** what I want you to know about people.*"

A friend of mine once said, "*People in the church would gossip less if they asked the Holy Spirit about people and not each other!*" I call those Thorntonisms because a lot of the things she says, are short, yet powerful.

The Bible says, in 2 Corinthians 5:16, "*Therefore from now on we recognize no one according to the flesh; even though we have known Christ according to the flesh, yet now we know Him in this way no longer."* This doesn't mean that we are not to ensure that we know who people are. We should definitely be aware of those who pretend to be one thing, but in actuality, are something else. However, many Christians, and non-Christians misinterpret what the Bible says about judging and say that we should never judge.

In Matthew 7:1-5, Jesus did say that we should not judge. However, if you take a closer look, these verses will show that He is referring to hypocritical judging. He went on to say that when a hypocrite cleans up his own life, then he will be fit to judge another. Of course, it is always wrong to make judgments about a person's motives or thoughts because we don't know their mind.

For example, in John 7:24, Jesus said, *"Stop judging by mere appearances, and make a right judgment."* In this verse Jesus is talking about making righteous judgments in regard to God's laws. We must make judgments in matters of biblical doctrine and righteous living. The Bible is our foundation and if we don't discern and follow what God says, then it will become just another book, and everyone will do whatever they think is right, just like the Israelites did in the time of the Judges. Judges 21:25 says, *"In those days Israel had no king; everyone did as he saw fit".*

To keep God's commands, we must first judge what is right and what is wrong. For example, 1 Cor. 5:11-13 says, *"... you must not associate with anyone who calls himself a brother but is sexually immoral or greedy, an idolater or a slanderer, a drunkard or a swindler. With such a man do not even eat. What business is it of mine to judge those outside the church? Are you not to judge those inside? God will judge those outside. 'Expel the wicked man from among you".* In these verses, God tells us to judge church members and expel them if necessary.

Then we are told in Rom. 12:9, *"Hate what is evil; cling to what is good."* How can we do that if we don't first judge what is good and what is evil? So, we must make judgments about what is right and what is wrong so that we can live according to God's commands.

This all means that, 'Yes', we are to judge, but we should never judge onto condemnation. We don't know who will repent or when they will repent. But one thing for sure, God knows the position of our hearts when we 'judge' someone's action, and if that position is not one of love, through Christ for the person, then we need to ask ourselves, why do we expect that same mercy from God that we do not offer another?

Alcohol: No Longer A Comforter

One of the things my mother taught me is that you say 'Good Morning' when you first see a person during the morning time, and you say 'Good Night' when you see them in the evening. It was all about being polite and ensuring that you are not considered rude by the people you are encountering.

Another way of addressing this issue of people acknowledging others when they walk into a room is *if a person walks into a room and doesn't say... Good Morning... or even Hello... you can bet that they did not wake up saying Good Morning to Jesus.*

On the other hand, God wants us to acknowledge everyone we encounter in order to acknowledge His image here on earth. So for me, saying good morning and good evening is something that I make sure I do with everyone. From the CEO and other executives to the cleaning crew, their presence will be acknowledged. Given this, I never knew how much of an impact that would have until I met Scott, a temporary security guard who worked at my office building.

Being that I grew up in the Bronx in New York City in the 70s and 80s, I can spot a drug addict or alcoholic from a mile away. Even better, since working on Wall Street for almost 20 years, I could spot functioning drug addicts and alcoholics as well.

The first time I saw Scott was when I was leaving the office late one night. He was laid back in the security guard's chair and as I passed through the security turn-style, I simply smiled and said 'Good Night'. He just glanced up at me a bit surprised that I spoke to him. For the next two to three days, I would say good night whenever I would leave the office and about the fourth day, as I came off the elevator, I noticed Scott would actually sit up straight in preparation for me to say 'Good Night' and give his response with a forced smile.

One Friday morning I entered the building and there was Scott. I said, "Good Morning!" A bit surprised to see him, and I also noticed that he was somewhat happy at my surprised response.

At the end of the day, my friend Lauren had come to pick me up. Even though we started at the company at the same time, she was placed in a different location from mine. She came to my office and waited for me to finish some tasks before heading out to dinner.

After we got off the elevator I realized that I had left something upstairs and proceeded to return my office while she waited downstairs. When I returned to the lobby, I saw her standing at the guard's desk talking to Scott. I knew she was talking to Scott of Jesus.

As I approached the desk, I heard her saying things that I had heard from so many Christians, that actually made me '*NOT WANT TO BE ONE*'. I won't go into all that was said but I am sure you could think of a few things.

While she was talking 'at him', he stopped her mid-sentence and looked at me and asked, "You are a real Christian aren't you?" I asked, "Why do you ask"? He said, "Oh, I know you are because in my week of working here you are the only one who smiled at me and acknowledged my existence with a Good Morning or Good Evening". At that point in time, I saw my friend's face turning red with anger.

I said to Scott, Yes, if you want to call me a Christian you can, but I consider myself someone who loves Jesus. He proceeded to tell us why he wasn't a Christian and why he didn't believe in God. After talking to him for a few more minutes, Lauren and I left and needless to say, we eventually were no longer friends.

The next time I saw Scott, it was the following week and yet again, I was leaving out of the office after 10pm. When he saw me get off of the elevator, he jumped up out of his seat and with a big smile asked, "Would you mind if I walk you to your car because it's so late and I am sure you parked in the parking structure because there are no more cars on the lot". Of course, I said yes and as he walked me to my car I bluntly told him that I knew he was a functioning alcoholic, but one day he is going to love Jesus Christ.

He proceeded to tell me about his father and other so-called Christians who were not very nice. He also explained to me how he got the knot on his forehead, which was from fighting, and that his love of alcohol was okay, because it wasn't hurting anyone.

As we walked, I proceeded to tell him that I knew he drank a lot of Vodka and of course with wide eyes he asked, "How did you know that?" I smiled and told him that God knows everything. I also told him that the reason he drank was because he was hurt and trying not to feel the pain, so it's easier to drink and be inebriated than feel the pain. As we continued to walk and talk, well, I did most of the talking, he just looked completely mystified.

Once we reached my brand-spanking new car, he marveled at the interior and shared how he loved cars. I told him to get into the car and I would drive him back to the building. While in the car he shared that he had never driven a brand new car and that he liked the smell. Once we got back to the building, I got out of the car that I had for less than a week and told him to take it for a spin.

Smiling now as I recall his face. He looked like a 10 year old little boy who just opened a Christmas gift he had waited all year to receive. He said, "No way"... "No way". I asked, "Why, because you are inebriated right now aren't you?" He said, "Yes". I said, "No worries, Jesus and angels will cover you and 'my' car." And I walked away to stand on the sidewalk. He stood in front of the open, driver-side door for a minute or two as I just stared at him. He finally got into the car and drove off.

As I waited for him to return, I don't remember praying, I don't remember feeling anything crazy. What I do remember was feeling excited about whatever God was doing in and with Scott while he was driving the car.[21]

Within about 10 minutes, Scott was driving back to the building with the biggest smile on his face. I asked, "So how was it, it feels amazing doesn't it?" He said, "You are the craziest black lady I have ever met in my life. You are either on drugs or really believe in this Jesus thing."

I smiled and briefly shared with him how I got saved. I also told him how all of my grandmother's sons, were, and still are alcoholics. I also asked him if I could pray that he didn't drink anymore and the taste for alcohol leaves him. At that point he started to laugh and said, "Now I know you are crazy!" Well, you know where this story is going.

The next day, I get to my office and I did not see Scott at the front desk, the regular security guard had returned. Later on during the afternoon, I got a knock on my office door and it was Scott. I was quite surprised to see him because I never saw security on our floor.

I welcomed him into the office and he sat down. I was smiling profusely at the fact that he was clearly uncomfortable. I asked him, "What's going on, to-what-do I owe this pleasure?" As he began to talk, I also noticed that there was more traffic outside of my office than usual as people were peeking into see why the security guard was in my office.

"What did you do to me?" "What do you mean, what did I do to you?" I responded. "You did something to me because last night, after I got home, I poured myself a drink and it didn't taste good. So, I got a beer and it tasted disgusting. I made a couple of mixed drinks to make the drinks stronger but nothing, NOTHING", he proclaimed.

I must admit, and I told him as well, that I too was surprised at the fact that God moved so fast. But I also realized that it was God working in tandem with Scott's desire not to be a functioning alcoholic. I also shared with him some other testimonies of God healing hearts and minds as well as delivering other men and women off of drugs and alcohol.

---

[21]NOTE: No one should drink and drive. However, I was following the leading of the Holy Spirit specifically for this person.

"What do I do now", Scott asked as he looked at me bewildered? I did not tell him to go to church, I did not tell him to find a pastor. I told him, "You need to get to know Jesus Christ so that you can know the one who died for your sins so you can have a real life here on earth, and a life with Jesus after you leave this earth." I shared with Scott that I had never invited anyone to church. I asked him if he had any questions, and told him that I would be happy to help him seek out the answers but I would pray for a man of God to come into his life in order to disciple him. The one thing I did tell him to do was to read the Bible. "Read and discover who Jesus is so that you can grow in the knowledge of Him. Especially because you have per-conceived notions on who He is because of the many 'bad' and 'false' individuals who proclaimed to represent Him."

After that meeting in my office, I saw Scott one more time and then he was gone. I was tempted to ask the permanent security guard for the placement agency's contact information in order to get in touch with Scott, but God stopped me and told me that my assignment with Scott was done.

What was my assignment with Scott? It was to show him the love of God by simply acknowledging his existence. By simply smiling and saying "Good Morning". In addition, letting him know that he is more valuable than an object that is fitted with a higher-output V-6 that boasts 295 horses and can go from 0-60 mph in 5.7 seconds. *Excuse me, I digressed.*

God's assignment for me, was to let me know that I was growing in my understanding of the authority I would walk in, as it related to helping people who were bound by alcoholism, and other addictions. Also, by letting them know that they 'are' worth something, give them hope, and help them to understand that God sees their worth, which is more than what they might see while looking in the mirror.

We must all have revelation of the truth that God sees our worth, from beginning to the end. He sees and has determined our worth because we look just like Him. But the challenge is, people feel worthless, not when others put little value on them, but when they choose to accept the value that others have determined.

People will often look at the quality of work, or the type of work, someone is doing, and if they're doing a poor job, or is a garbage man, versus a doctor, then people will view these two people with different value sets. We all know that this is not the correct way of seeing value in someone. If we truly saw the value in people as God does, we would treat people differently...regardless of their status.

Ask yourself, what value have you put on others, and an even more important question, what value have you accepted for yourself that others have put on you? I say put because they can present, or try to apply a value to you that does not come from God. It is entirely up to you to reject it and fully accept the value God has placed on you.

"Therefore I tell you, do not be anxious about your life, what you will eat or what you will drink, nor about your body, what you will put on. Is not life more than food, and the body more than clothing? Look at the birds of the air: they neither sow nor reap nor gather into barns, and yet your heavenly Father feeds them. Are you not of more value than they? And which of you by being anxious can add a single hour to his span of life? And why are you anxious about clothing? Consider the lilies of the field, how they grow: they neither toil nor spin, yet I tell you, even Solomon in all his glory was not arrayed like one of these. Matthew 6:25-34 ESV

The Message version puts verses 25-26 this way, *"If you decide for God, living a life of God-worship, it follows that you don't fuss about what's on the table at mealtimes or whether the clothes in your closet are in fashion. There is far more to your life than the food you put in your stomach, more to your outer appearance than the clothes you hang on your body. Look at the birds, free and unfettered, not tied down to a job description, careless in the care of God. And you count far more to him than birds.*

Think about it, you are made in the image of God. You have a savior who died and was resurrected for you. Given such, you can't put a price on yourself, and you should never let someone else attempt to do so either. The key to seeing and understanding your value, and the value of others, is to see our value in light of the one who created us.

Helen and the Navigation System

I had just bought a brand-new 2007 sports sedan. Some friends and I drove to a church in South Carolina in order to spend New Year's Eve and a day surrounded by people who were seeking God. During our time, there were a number of supernatural incidences, a lot of good, and some bad that will have me forever thankful that I love Jesus. But the point of this story is to share how walking in obedience to God is not only required of you, but you should also require it of those you associate with as well.

Almost all of us grew up hearing, "Birds of the same feather, flock together." This saying means that you are usually friends with people who are similar to you. If you are with people who use profanity, you also use profanity. If you are with people who enjoy helping others, then you are most likely someone who likes to help others as well. I wasn't sure why I did not realize this prior to being saved. But because of the lie, that "you must love everyone, and you should never shun anyone," that most churches preach, I went through a phase of allowing everyone into my life. There were people who had serious issues that I thought I had to allow into my life because not giving then access would mean that I was a 'bad Christian'. However, I have learned that you must have boundaries in your life in order to not only protect your family, your own peace, and happiness, but it is only the grace of God that will allow you to have people in your life that you are supposed to help have the same freedom you fought for. God will make it perfectly clear who is supposed to be in your life, that He sent...versus an assignment that the enemy has sent into your life to bring confusion and destruction.

There is a story in the Bible about Achan that clearly shows how God sees those who are not walking in obedience to Him, even if they are part of a large community. In addition, there are a number of scriptures where God makes it clear, "How can two walk together, unless they agree?" (Amos 3:3)

Despite the fact that the people I was traveling to South Carolina with had major rage issues, and needed to be delivered, I knew that I was supposed to spend New Year's Eve with this friend and a married couple. I later learned why.

After the conference was over, my friend Helen and I were in my car heading back to Georgia, while the husband and wife were heading back to the state in which they lived. We had already said our goodbyes to friends we made while at the church and, I for one was ready to get back to my home.

The car we were in had a $2000+ navigation and audio system. I needed to say the cost of the system because of what I am about to share. As we were on the highway, about 30 minutes away from the church, I began to feel like something was wrong.

As I began to pray, the navigation system began to blink in and out, as if someone was turning it off and on. Then, the map started spinning and indicated that I needed to get off at the next exit. Upon getting off the next exit, which was simply to get back onto the highway and go back in the direction we left, the navigation was fine. But, I thought to myself, that couldn't be right. So, I ignored the navigation system, got off the next exit in order to continue in the direction heading back to Georgia.

After getting back on the highway, the navigation system did the same thing, it directed me to get off the next exit and the directions were taking us back towards the church.

But this time, I ignored the directions to get off the exit and continued on the highway. At that point, the navigation system lights started to go dim and then finally the screen went completely black.

I looked at my friend and asked, "Was there something you were supposed to do back at the church before we left?" She looked at me wide-eyed and said "Yes". I was... HIGHLY ANNOYED!

I stated that, "The reason the navigation is going out is because you were supposed to take care of something before we left, and you knew it." She disagreed that the reason the navigation system wasn't working was because of her. But as I took the next exit ramp in order to head back to the church, the navigation turned back on with the direction going back to the church without me having to type in the church's address.

It is not my main intent to make this book all about different theological approaches to scripture or even exegete them, but we must understand scripture as it relates to walking with those who are not walking in obedience to God.

The first story where we see disobedience is The Fall, which is where Adam and Eve disobeyed God as it relates to not eating from the Tree of Knowledge of Good and Evil. But most people tend to judge God for judging Achan so severely when Achan sinned, and it affected Israel.

The story of Achan's sin and God's punishment is found in the book of Joshua 7. Achan was an Israelite who fought the battle of Jericho with Joshua. God had directed the Israelites to terminate the entire city of Jericho because of its great sin. Only Rahab the harlot and her household were spared because she had hidden the Israelite spies. God further commanded that, unlike most victories when soldiers were allowed to take the spoils, the Israelites were to take nothing from Jericho. Everything in it was "accursed" or "devoted to destruction." God warned that anyone taking spoils from Jericho would "make the camp of Israel liable to destruction and bring trouble on it" (Joshua 6:18-19). The Israelites obeyed, except for Achan, who stole a robe, some gold and silver, and hid them in his tent.

When his sin was discovered, God commanded that Achan and his entire family, and all his possessions be destroyed, a punishment that seems very harsh to us today. While we are troubled that Achan's family and household were killed with him, we must keep in mind the communal aspect of ancient Israelite life. One's actions affected one's family, for good or bad. Think about it this way, Rahab's actions saved her entire family, while Achan's actions destroyed his.

It is clear in the story that sin caused God's blessing upon the Israelites to be withheld in their battle against the city of Ai, and the Israelites "were routed by the men of Ai, who killed about thirty-six of them" (Joshua 7:4-5). Thirty-six innocent people died because of Achan's sin. He stole that which was "devoted to destruction" and so brought destruction on others. God explained to Joshua, *"That is why the Israelites could not stand against their enemies; they turned their backs and ran because they had been made liable to destruction"* (Joshua 7:12).

It is amazing, how people think that when they sin, and disobey God, it only affects them individually.

Also, the gold and silver that were stolen, were stolen from God Himself. The metals were to be added to the treasury of the Lord, and, in stealing them, Achan robbed God directly. Achan's disobedience was also an insult to God's holiness and His right to command His people accordingly. Even though God gave Achan a night to consider his sin and come to Him in repentance, Achan did not run to receive God's grace and mercy.

The gold and silver which Achan stole had a stronger pull on his heart... and ultimately, his commitment to God.

There are a number of stories I can tell, where, the mishaps or negative outcomes were associated with people that I was surrounded by, prior to being saved, and unfortunately, while being saved. I must also share, I did not learn my lesson, after the *navigation system* event.

However, it is a lesson that I have since learned, despite the fact that some churches constantly promote that we are to 'love everyone and be in relationship with everyone'... even though the many Bible verses that say otherwise.[22]

We must understand that God sees sin, notwithstanding the fact that you might also have heard, "God can't look upon sin." God did not see faith in Achan's heart. Instead Achan did not only disobey, he was a nonbeliever. Walking in unbelief and rebellion will eventually bring death to oneself; to the things they are trying to succeed at, and sometimes, death to those and the things others might be trying to succeed at as well.

Some will also say that the story of Achan was 'before' Jesus. Yes, this is indeed true, but God does not change. He is a holy God and hates sin. He must punish sin, but He is also a loving God. On one hand His love desires to bless man. On the other hand, His holiness says, "I must judge sin." How is it possible for the two to be brought together?

Thank you God for Jesus Christ. God's plan whereby people who were/are sinners may be brought into the presence of God and not be under Divine condemnation, because of Jesus Christ.

When Jesus Christ died on the cross, He took the punishment for our sins so that we could be forgiven. Jesus deserved no punishment for He had never sinned. It is as if we were on the cross, receiving the consequences that our sins deserved. But Jesus went to the cross, and died on the cross, for us. And because He did, we are justified, and

---

[22]Do two walk together unless they have agreed to do so? (Amos 3:3). Do not be deceived: "Bad company ruins good morals." (1 Corinthians 15:33). Whoever walks with the wise becomes wise, but the companion of fools will suffer harm. (Proverbs 13:20). But now I am writing to you not to associate with anyone who bears the name of brother if he is guilty of sexual immorality or greed, or is an idolater, reviler, drunkard, or swindler—not even to eat with such a one. (1 Corinthians 5:11). Do not be unequally yoked with unbelievers. For what partnership has righteousness with lawlessness? Or what fellowship has light with darkness? (2 Corinthians 6:14). Do not associate with a man given to anger; Or go with a hot-tempered man, 25Or you will learn his ways And find a snare for yourself....(Proverbs 22:24)

proclaimed righteous. He took our sin, He took our death; He gave us righteousness and life. And like Achan, who God gave an opportunity to receive mercy and grace, Jesus is also offering to everyone, His mercy and grace.

Directions: Navigation System vs. God

Two years prior to the *Helen and the Navigation System* story, I had another navigation system issue, this time it was not associated with anyone but, me, myself and I.

Every New Yorker knows that if you are *not* told by a Californian, "No one walks in California", you won't know that you would need to buy a car once you move to certain parts of Southern California. Once God moved me to California, I thought I would simply hop on a bus, or train in order to get back and forth from work and home, but to my surprise, I needed to buy a car.

Still less than a year being saved, I prayed about which car I should get, without actually listening to hear what God was directing me to do. Why? I had my heart set on 'one' specific car.

The first car I test drove was a very nice, and luxurious, used BMW 745, my dream car. As I drove around with the salesman, an older Korean gentleman, he asked me how many people were in my family. I told him that it was just me and to which he replied in a very strong Korean accent, "You don't need suchee big kah for one person, you should get yourself-uh smalla kah." I wasn't thinking about my expenses or income, I was simply thinking that I wanted 'that' car. But wisdom took over and I ended up buying a brand new, smaller car.

Similar to the other car discussed earlier, this car also had a $2000+ navigation and audio system. This was one feature that I made sure that I purchased, being that I 'thought' I would need the navigation system, in order to find my way around, not only the areas where I worked and lived in, but get to the areas that 'God would guide me to'. Did you catch that I needed a navigation system so that GOD could guide me? Now, even though that was my thinking, I fell into trusting the navigation system more than the voice of the Lord.

I cannot count the number of times when the Holy Spirit was leading me to get off of the highway, and yet the navigation was indicating that I should go straight. Every time I ignored the Holy Spirit, I ran into either traffic, or delays due to an accident. It did not take me long to learn this and, again, I cannot count how many times I was protected from either dealing with traffic, or a major car accident.

There was one incident that comes to mind as it relates to obeying His leading versus the navigation system. I was on my way to a conference to see a speaker teach on deliverance. I honestly did not feel that I was ready to see this person and was quite surprised when God told me to go and see him.

He was based in another state and I thought that I would have to fly to the location of his ministry. But when God told me to go and see him, I did my research and discovered that the minister was going to only be a two hour drive away, versus the almost four hour flight that I would have taken to his headquarters.

While driving to the conference, I clearly heard the Lord say, "***Pull over and wait.***" After pulling over, I called a friend and told her what was happening. We prayed and thanked God for whatever He was protecting me from. As I pulled off of the shoulder in order to continue driving, within 10 minutes, I passed a motorcycle and a few cars piled up from an accident. The cars that were part of the pile up were cars that I was driving along with as I made my way to the conference. Why did He protect me and not the other drivers? Why was I protected during a number of incidents that I know He guided me out of? I can honestly say, and be 100% certain that I don't know the answer.

I believe Psalms 121:6-8, and all scriptures that talk about God protecting us.

The sun will not smite you by day, nor the moon by night. 7The LORD will protect you from all evil; He will keep your soul. 8The LORD will guard your going out and your coming in From this time forth and forever. (Psalms 121:6-8)

You are my hiding place; you will protect me from trouble and surround me with songs of deliverance. (Psalms 32:7)

The LORD protects and preserves them-- they are counted among the blessed in the land-- he does not give them over to the desire of their foes. (Psalm 41:2)

...no harm will overtake you, no disaster will come near your tent. (Psalm 91:10)

No harm overtakes the righteous, but the wicked have their fill of trouble. (Proverbs 12:21)

Even though there are these scriptures above as well as so many others that reveal how God protects us, why do accidents happen? Why do innocent people die before their time? I have had a couple of accidents, and after being saved, I knew, without a shadow of a doubt which ones were associated with the enemy trying to kill me. From a demon possessed man trying to run me off the road, to a woman who ran a red light, plowing into my driver-side door and then proclaiming that I hit her, I can go into details that would make someone feel like they are reading a script for an action movie. But, even with those various situations, I cannot count the number of times when I was protected while on the road, in the air, or in a country where Christians were not welcomed. Even from perverted men following me on the streets, God is true to His word. And for those who feel another way about God being true to His word, I implore you to discontinue apportioning blame onto Him, and apply it to the one that comes to kill, steal, and destroy.

Helen's Bank Fees and Thailand's Tithes

Walking in covenant with people who are not in covenant with God can have lasting effects on various parts of your life. In addition, engaging in a business with people whose focus is on taking advantage of others and earning money, versus helping people and earning money, will 'always' have a negative outcome.

I will not go into all the details here as it relates to the idol...excuse me, the one thing most Christians still deal with, and that is money. However, the entire Bible is 100% clear on giving, helping, serving, and being like Jesus, when it comes to your time and money.

One day, at 4:14pm to be exact, Helen called to confess that she let worrying about finances contribute to her making a decision that she knew did *not* please God. She received a check for about $80, which was all the money she had due to various circumstances. She went to the bank to deposit the money but realized that she had unknowingly bounced a check and had a negative balance of $49.

She went to another bank to open up another account in order to avoid paying the $49. But as she walked out of the new bank with the new account, the Holy Spirit began to convict her. So, when she called me she said, "Oh Lord, I did something with a wrong spirit!" After she explained the situation, I kindly said, "I understand the whole 'confess our sins to one another' but you know what you need to do." As I was saying that, she was walking back to the bank where she owed the $49. By 7:00 pm, someone had given her $50 and while she was sharing with me how she received the money, our call was interrupted with a call from someone offering her a job which started the next day. Would she have received the call if she did not pay the overdue balance? We don't know. But what I do know is, I would rather have peace with God than a new bank account with money in it. But because we love God, we can have peace with Him and money in the bank.

I do not know anyone who does not have Jesus and yet, have peace in their life with all the money they have. Yes, I know wealthy people, those who are saved and those who know nothing about Jesus. But every single one who is saved and wealthy, if they lost all their money tomorrow, they will still be praising Jesus. However, those whose money, is their god, would not be okay if they lost it all.

Even though Helen did not have money at the time, she knew that the peace of God was worth more than a few dollars. I also know individuals who have an illusion of peace, even when they are not doing what God told them to do. Their illusion of peace comes from the amount of money they have in their accounts.

An example of this is when I was in another country, visiting some friends. The husband's family is pretty wealthy, well, quite wealthy and we had just spent an evening at an amazing restaurant in one of the best hotels in the city. The food was wonderful, the ambiance was amazing, and it is simply part of the lifestyle of the wealthy.

As soon as we walked into their very large, three bedrooms, three bathrooms, luxury apartment, ½ way in, I blurted out, "You guys have not paid your tithes have you?" It was as if the words by-passed my mind and came right out of my mouth.

They stopped midway into the apartment, and the wife said, "Well, we haven't found a ministry we want to join yet..." and some other things that I can't and don't want to remember. But I do remember telling them that they do not have to spend any of God's money on me in any shape or form while I was there. And, Achan's story just kept replaying in my mind till I left the country.

Needless to say, the experience with this couple, which was the same couple that Helen and I were with while in South Carolina, was the beginning of my encountering a number of people who simply wanted all that God came with and not God himself.

Walking in obedience with God isn't simply doing what He wants us to do. It is having a deep desire to become all that He desires for us to become and that is to look like Jesus. God wants us to love Him for Him, not for His things, His gifts, signs, wonders, bank accounts, or cars. When it comes to walking into all that He calls us to walk in, may it be the way we love, or our destiny, we must make sure that we are walking with those He has assigned to us for the season we are in.

Before closing out, *Stumbling and Getting Back Up*, it must be noted that God will indeed, for a season, have you walking alongside those who don't want Him. They may be angry, and bitter, but need His love the most. You might be honored, by Him to represent a natural manifestation of His love, grace, and mercy to the person that you know is demonized, jealous of you, or even gossips about you. But at the end of your life, if you can look back without any anger, hate, or bitterness toward those who did not receive you, with love and compassion in your heart for them, then you truly represented Him well. Because in actuality, they were not rejecting you, they were rejecting the One who sent you.

"Whoever listens to you listens to me; whoever rejects you rejects me; but whoever rejects me rejects him who sent me." Luke 10:16

Footsteps Ordered

He Will Not Forsake His Saints

Do not fret because of those who are evil or be envious of those who do wrong; 2 for like the grass they will soon wither, like green plants they will soon die away.

3 Trust in the Lord and do good; dwell in the land and enjoy safe pasture.

4 Take delight in the Lord, and he will give you the desires of your heart.

5 Commit your way to the Lord; trust in him and he will do this:

6 He will make your righteous reward shine like the dawn, your vindication like the noonday sun.

7 Be still before the Lord and wait patiently for him; do not fret when people succeed in their ways, when they carry out their wicked schemes.

8 Refrain from anger and turn from wrath; do not fret—it leads only to evil.

9 For those who are evil will be destroyed, but those who hope in the Lord will inherit the land.

10 A little while, and the wicked will be no more; though you look for them, they will not be found.

11 But the meek will inherit the land and enjoy peace and prosperity.

12 The wicked plot against the righteous and gnash their teeth at them;

13 but the Lord laughs at the wicked, for he knows their day is coming.

14 The wicked draw the sword and bend the bow to bring down the poor and needy, to slay those whose ways are upright.

15 But their swords will pierce their own hearts, and their bows will be broken.

16 Better the little that the righteous have than the wealth of many wicked;

17 for the power of the wicked will be broken, but the Lord upholds the righteous.

18 The blameless spend their days under the Lord's care, and their inheritance will endure forever.

19 In times of disaster they will not wither; in days of famine they will enjoy plenty.

20 But the wicked will perish: Though the Lord's enemies are like the flowers of the field, they will be consumed, they will go up in smoke.

21 The wicked borrow and do not repay, but the righteous give generously;

22 those the Lord blesses will inherit the land, but those he curses will be destroyed.

23 The Lord makes firm the steps of the one who delights in him;

24 though he may stumble, he will not fall, for the Lord upholds him with his hand.

25 I was young and now I am old, yet I have never seen the righteous forsaken or their children begging bread.

26 They are always generous and lend freely; their children will be a blessing.

27 Turn from evil and do good; then you will dwell in the land forever.

28 For the Lord loves the just and will not forsake his faithful ones. Wrongdoers will be completely destroyed; the offspring of the wicked will perish.

29 The righteous will inherit the land and dwell in it forever.

30 The mouths of the righteous utter wisdom, and their tongues speak what is just.

31 The law of their God is in their hearts; their feet do not slip.

32 The wicked lie in wait for the righteous, intent on putting them to death;

33 but the Lord will not leave them in the power of the wicked or let them be condemned when brought to trial.

34 Hope in the Lord and keep his way. He will exalt you to inherit the land; when the wicked are destroyed, you will see it.

35 I have seen a wicked and ruthless man flourishing like a luxuriant native tree,

36 but he soon passed away and was no more; though I looked for him, he could not be found.

37 Consider the blameless, observe the upright; a future awaits those who seek peace.

38 But all sinners will be destroyed; there will be no future for the wicked.

39 The salvation of the righteous comes from the Lord; he is their stronghold in time of trouble.

40 The Lord helps them and delivers them; he delivers them from the wicked and saves them, because they take refuge in him. (Psalms 37:1-40)

Understanding Forgiveness

I had been physically assaulted while vacationing in Miami with my cousin and some friends. The events that took place that day are detailed in *Forgiveness Understanding God's Grace and Mercy*, © therefore going into details here is not needed. However, God telling me to forgive the man who assaulted me was another level of obedience that even I, at the time did not know if I was ready for.

I had been offered a position in California, but before relocating from New York, I had to spend some time with a relocation specialist in order to search for an apartment. While searching for a place to call home, I had to suffer, by staying at the Ritz-Carlton, a luxury hotel that was situated on 23-acre grounds, in an upmarket neighborhood. It was located about two miles from The Huntington Library, Art Collections, and Botanical Gardens, and about an ½hr drive from Rodeo Drive, Beverly Hills.

While in California for the week, meeting with members of the team I would be working with, as well as looking for a place to stay, I had received a call indicating that the trial for the assault was going to take place that following Monday in Florida.

I had arranged with the prosecuting attorney that I would fly from California to Florida, have the necessary meetings, and then fly back to

New York. It was set, almost two years of waiting for the case to go to court, it was all finally coming to an end. I could not believe that I was closing out that chapter and starting a new one all at the same time. However, God had other things in mind as it related to closing out that chapter.

As I sat waiting for my dinner to arrive to my room, I heard the Lord say, "***Forgive him and don't go!***" I couldn't believe what I was hearing. But, I knew it was the Lord.

I called the prosecuting attorney and told him that I was not going to go to Florida for the case and I had forgiven the man. He couldn't believe what I was saying. He then said everything that was already in my head prior to calling: "What will everyone say?" "What will everyone think?" "They would think I wanted it to happen"... and everything someone who has been a victim of an assault would think!

As I listened to him rant on the phone, in the end, he said, "Well he has daughters, I wonder how he is going to feel when this happens to them?" I knew at that point that I would pray for this man's daughters, whose father's name I don't remember, whose face, God has wiped from my memory, and who I hope to see in heaven.

Forgiving individuals who have gossiped about you and/or used you for various reasons is not just a mental decision. It is a decision of your will to obey God's command to forgive.

Sometimes, the mental acts of obedience are the hardest ones to fulfill. Why? Because you have to completely surrender your will and desire to feel hurt, bitter, or like a victim, to Jesus Christ. It is the power that resides in you that empowers you to forgive, and walk in forgiveness.

If your heart is fully surrendered to God, and you are living a life of love, peace, and joy, it doesn't stop people from hurting you, knowingly and unknowingly. Sometimes, it appears, as if, the happier you are, the angrier people become. But we should know that it is the enemy 'in them' that they have *given permission* to rule their heart.

In addition, being completely enamored with Him does not stop you from feeling the hurt that comes with betrayal. But one thing is certain, the hurt does not hurt for long, nor does it hurt as deep as it would if you did not have Jesus in your life. Get ready, a band-aid is about to be ripped off; *most of the time, you are simply offended by someone who did not do what you thought they should do, or they didn't do it the way you wanted them to do it. You're hurt because you have an issue of being offended, and that has nothing to do with the person, it all has to do with you.*

I was asked by a few friends, "Why don't you get angry?" I didn't understand what they were getting at, and they knew it. One proceeded to recall a couple of situations where someone else would have responded in anger, or at least voiced their disdain towards the person.

The thing is, I do not shy away from letting people know when they are 'out of order'. I thank God for people in my life who can pull my coattails to my disposition that they believe needs to be adjusted. However, I have this saying, "Take 5 minutes and cry it out. When you are done, keep moving." Some people don't like this stance because they believe that I lack compassion and understanding, which is far from the truth.

I have been crying since I was saved. Whenever I see someone hurt, in pain, grieving, or in sorrow, my entire being grieves. However, when someone is attacked, verbally, with gossip, or lies, and they want to wallow in their pain, where their pain becomes their identity, I refuse to take part in it. Unfortunately, this is how most people, Christians, and non-Christians live.

They live in a world made up of all the bad things done to them, by loved ones, or even strangers. And yet, refuse to understand, why they have no peace, love, or consistent joy in their lives. How can we, say we love God, and yet, the same grace and mercy He gives us, we don't extend to others? Whether they deserve it or not, we didn't deserve what we received either. Meaning we did nothing to 'earn' it, and yet, we believe that others must earn grace and mercy from us.

I refuse to house emotions that won't last for eternity in God's kingdom. Every emotion, attitude, and disposition, that lasts for eternity in hell, are those associated with hate, jealousy, bitterness, lust, fear, etc., none of which I want to live temporarily or eternally experiencing.

We will experience emotions in heaven. Emotions like love and joy because we are in God's presence forever. The Bible says that heaven's inhabitants declare to one another, *"Let us rejoice and be glad and give him glory!"* (Revelation 19:7).

Should you, or rather, will you continue to allow emotions like anger, hatred, and doubt to control you? Or will you allow heaven's peace to rule in your heart, a peace so strong that it keeps emotions like anger and bitterness away? To put it another way, wouldn't all of our lives be better if we could banish emotions that destroy us? Some believe that it is not possible. However, when we put our lives, emotions included, in the hands of Jesus Christ, and give him permission to fill us with His Spirit, then it is possible, actually, guaranteed that we will live and walk in the fruit of the Spirit.

The Bible says, "But the fruit of the Spirit is love, joy, peace, patience, kindness, goodness, faithfulness, gentleness and self-control" (Galatians 5:22-23). By faith we open our heart to Christ's transforming power. But it is walking in obedience to Him, that the Holy Spirit is continuously given permission to manifest His fruit through us.

Coffee...My Holy Spirit

When God asks you a question, it's normally because 'you think' you know the answer when in actuality you don't. One day while enjoying a 'triple grande no foam extra hot latte' with one packet of an artificial sweetener and one packet of brown sugar, God said, "**You are addicted to coffee!**" To which I responded, "No I am not." (Pause and take time to shake your head and laugh at my foolery).

I felt as though He said, "*You can't go one week without drinking coffee!*" As I was sipping on my deliciously roasted cup of java, I reasoned that I only drank one cup of coffee a day. Granted it was a 'grande', I nursed the entire day. I had a process.

I drank about a 1/3 of it during the morning as I checked emails and accomplished different tasks that needed to be completed before the afternoon. During the afternoon, I rarely had lunch because I wasn't hungry due to the fact that I sipped on my coffee until it got luck warm. Then I would take it to the microwave, nuke it until it was piping hot and then finish every little bit while completing other tasks. Not only because I enjoyed the taste of coffee but the cost of it contributed to me not wanting to waste any.

As I drove home that day, I said to myself, "I could stop drinking coffee"...no problem. Until the next day, during the afternoon, I grrr

WANTED grrr coffee! (grrr represents growling). I thought this is not possible, I can't be addicted to coffee. It's not crack, cocaine, weed, alcohol, or any other drug that I had seen so many people addicted to. But there I was, not having withdrawal systems like headaches or body aches... God is good that way. But I did realize that I wanted coffee and I wanted it bad. Thus, what's a girl to do... pray!

As I prayed during the day, I realized that I was praying, not for God to help me with my desire for coffee, but I was repenting for having a strong desire for something that I was putting above God. There should be no idols of any sort in our lives where we desire a thing or person, more than God. In actuality, when God points out that we have made a person or thing an idol, and yet we make excuses for loving our children more than anything, or loving our spouse above loving and obeying God, then there is a major issue. Some call it a problem, but God calls this sin.

When we read the Bible, there is one consistent issue addressed, and that is idolatry. References abound in connection with Israel's struggle with the gods of their neighbors and gods that were created by man. The children of Israel gave into the temptation to conform to the values of other tribes that they neighbored, versus walking with, and according to how God directed. What is interesting to mention is that God, who says, He is holy, told the Israelites to be holy. Why is this worth mentioning? The Hebrew meaning for "holy" is "different" or "apartness."

To be in a personal relationship with God, is to recognize Him for who He is. Unless He is preeminent in our heart, our relationship with God will suffer. To elevate anything or anyone to the same level as God in our heart is to bring division in our relationship with Him and diminish our experience of His power and presence.

Here is the thing, it wasn't the fact that I was drinking coffee, Monday-Friday. And for the record, I did not drink coffee on the weekends. It wasn't something that I had planned, it just happened to be that way. It was the *comfort* that I did not realize I was receiving every time I had a cup. I did not realize that I was being comforted by the smell and even the taste of coffee. It wasn't the caffeine, but the 'experience' that brought me something that I did not realize I needed.

After a week of not going to my favorite coffee dealer, I was driving home happy that God, in His goodness was giving me revelation as to why He told me to stop drinking coffee. Smiling and loving His presence, I knew that drinking coffee wasn't something I wanted to do if it was something that I was allowing to comfort me, outside of Him.

As I was having these thoughts, and driving down the Ventura freeway, there were no houses, no stores, nothing, except other cars. However, during the midst of these thoughts, the strong smell of coffee floated into my car! Yes, the windows were closed, the A/C was on, and there were no old coffee cups in my car. Even if the windows were opened, there was no way the smell of coffee should have been entering my car.

At that point, I started praying and laughing while rebuking whatever spirit that was attempting to mock me and entice me. At that point in time, I knew that idol was defeated.

About a week or two later, I was in my apartment, leaning against my wall typing out a paper for school. It was about 10:30 at night and I had a long night ahead of me. In a still small voice, I heard, "*Go get yourself a cup of coffee and* **enjoy.**" At first, I thought, 'wait, is this a trick?' I waited for a few minutes, and I felt that it was God saying to me, "I am not here to take anything from you that you enjoy, but if you make them an idol, then it is you I am protecting by having you rid yourself of them." I started to cry and rejoice in the fact that I knew God knew that He had my heart… and my taste buds.

After about 15 minutes, He told me to go to a specific coffee shop. I, yet again, reasoned that the shop would be closed and there was no way I would be able to get the 'triple grande no foam extra hot latte'. Nonetheless, I headed to the coffee shop, in my pajamas.

Once I reached the coffee shop, there was one guy in the shop, and he had just locked the door as I was getting out of my car. As I approached the door, he came back and opened it. I said, "I take it you are closed, sorry to bother you." He said, "Oh, no worries, I can make you a cup if you want, I haven't shut down the machines yet?" My heart leaped with excitement. He looked at me like I was weird but the delightful type of weird, not the crazy type of weird.

As he started to make the coffee, I shared with him how I was in school earning a Ph.D. and was going to be up all night doing research for a paper. He simply smiled as he continued making the coffee. I was also waiting for the slightest bit of, 'this is the enemy trying to trick me vibe'. But it never came.

What did come was, not one, but *TWO Triple Grande No Foam Extra Hot Lattes*! I looked at him as he put them in the pickup area. I was speechless. He said, "Go ahead, take them, they are on me!" I asked, "Are you sure? I can pay you, it's not a problem?" He simply smiled and said, "***Enjoy!***" Needless to say I started crying and smiling. But walked out of the coffee-shop because I did not want the 'delightful weird' to turn into 'crazy weird'.

When I arrived home, I sat on the floor, leaned against the wall, and drank my coffee with the presence of the Lord surrounding me. *For the first time I realized that He doesn't want us to choose between His goodness and something else. It is the something else that is good because of His goodness.* And before you ask, no the coffee did not keep me up all night. Actually, after I drank the coffee, wrote a little more, I went right to sleep.

But that wasn't the end of my coffee escapades. After leaving California and moving to Georgia, one day while serving at the prayer center, I heard the Lord say, "***Ask Maggie to pray for you and coffee.***" I thought, wait God, didn't we deal with this issue over a year ago. What is going on? But in obedience, I ran out to Maggie and stopped her from getting into her car and asked, "Maggie, by any chance, do you like coffee?" She turned her face up and said, "No, I think that stuff is disgusting!" I started to laugh and cry while explaining to her what had happened in California up until the point of me asking her if she liked coffee.

We both realized that there was something else associated with coffee that God wanted me to deal with and all of the issues were unresolved the first go around. God knew that I wasn't ready to deal with it when He first started dealing with me and my coffee issue.

As she prayed and I agreed with her prayer, we both focused on asking God to reveal what was the deeper issue. As I drove home, I realized that it was more than a coffee issue because unlike in California where I was going into the office every day, in Georgia, I was working from home and did not even have a coffee maker in my home.

Then one day in a vision, I saw myself sitting on my grandmother's lap and we were dipping our biscuits into coffee, having a good ole' time. I could feel her arms around me and I was well aware that my legs were dangling as I sat on her lap. I could feel the warmth of her skin against mine, and the thing that stood out the most was how happy, safe, and loved I felt. And that was it! Everything that God is and should be apprehended by anyone who trusts in Him, I was associating it with my grandmother. I often wondered why I only drank coffee Monday-Friday, whenever I was going into the office. It was a way for me to feel safe, love and protected from all the issues associated with working where I worked.

Since I started working on Wall Street, for the most part, I was always the only young, African-American woman working with predominately, wealthy white middle age, and older males. There are a number of stories I could share, but I have written about them in detail in my book, *Poor Girl, Smart Girl, Party Girl, God's Girl.*©

I realized that it was a way for me to feel protected, and at peace, while working in a non-peaceful environment. But then I remembered, that I had a routine of making sure that I had a hot cup of coffee during every meeting, or at least, prior to meetings. I did not realize that even after being saved, it was a habit that needed to be broken. It was great to have a grandmother who loved me and protected me. However, the problem with associating safety and love with my grandmother, and not with Jesus had to cease. I needed to ensure that it was only Jesus who provided those things. And, He didn't cost $5.

In you, Lord, I have taken refuge; let me never be put to shame. 2 In your righteousness, rescue me and deliver me; turn your ear to me and save me. 3Be my rock of refuge, to which I can always go; give the command to save me, for you are my rock and my fortress. 4 Deliver me, my God, from the hand of the wicked, from the grasp of those who are evil and cruel. 5 For you have been my hope, Sovereign Lord, my confidence since my youth. 6 From birth I have relied on you; you brought me forth from my mother's womb. I will ever praise you. 7 I have become a sign to many; you are my strong refuge. 8 My mouth is filled with your praise, declaring your splendor all day long. (Psalm 71, NIV)

He Protects My Nails

Walking in obedience, isn't always about 'don't do this, or don't do that,' sometimes, actually, most times, God wants to bless you. There are quite a number of occasions where I knew that God was teaching me that it wasn't always about other people, but it was Him wanting to bless me as well.

There was a day when I had meetings scheduled throughout the entire day. Once I reached my office and sat in my chair, I heard the Lord say, "**Go get your nails done**." I thought, wait a minute, don't you see my schedule for the day? As I began to sip on my coffee and prepare for the meetings, notifications for all the meetings began popping up indicating that the meetings were canceled. I was now free to leave my office in order to find a nail salon to get my nails done. As I drove around trying to see where He wanted me to go, I ended up in a quaint nail salon not too far from the office.

As I sat and got a manicure, I felt like I was supposed to go to a particular department store after I allowed my nails to dry. However, while the manicurist was polishing my nails, I had this sudden urgency to leave the salon as soon as she was done.

To be clear, if you ask any of my friends and family, they will all tell you that I do not like shopping. Actually, during that time in my walk with the Lord, still pretty new, I did not like crowds given the spiritual overload of picking up everything that was going on with people I was near. But nonetheless, I finished my manicure, 'wet nails' and all, and drove towards the department store.

When I got to the street to turn into the department store's parking facility, I felt like I had to go around the block, before turning into the garage. So, I went past the entrance of the garage and proceeded to go around the block. As I was approaching the parking garage entrance again, I saw on the right side of the street, the garage was on the left side, a woman trying to help hold up an older woman who was slumping to the ground.

There were a few people who saw what was going on, but they 'all' walked right past the two women. There were cars that were passing by, and slowing down only to see what was happening, but no one stopped to help.

I immediately pulled over to the right side of the street, jumped out of my car, and ran over to help. The younger woman was the older woman's daughter. The older lady had thought that she could walk without her walker, but her legs gave out and she wasn't able to move. Her daughter was trying to get her to hold on to the fence so that she could go, and get the car. After grabbing hold of the mom, her daughter went to get the car.

As we waited, her mother proceeded to ask me, "Are you an angel?" I said, "No I am not an angel because angels don't get married, have sex, and I want to do both and have children, so I am definitely not an angel." She and I both laughed hysterically as we waited. She also said, "I know God brought you here and He knew this was going to happen. He is always prepared to help us even when we make dumb decisions." As I tried to keep her from falling and listen to her talk, her daughter appeared five minutes later.

At this point, the woman couldn't move her legs at all, so we had to pick her up and carry her to the car. After putting her in the car, she looked at me and asked for my name. I told her that my name wasn't important.

Her daughter couldn't stop crying and being thankful for the help. I told her if they had time, I would tell them the story as to how I ended up there, but I didn't.

As I got back into my car to head to the office, I couldn't wait to share with my admins, who were of other religions, what had happened. As I was driving back, Holy Spirit said, "*Look at your nails.*" As I looked down, not a smudge or chip. Needless to say, I cried all the way back to my office.

This would be one of many times that I was either in a salon or spa, and God showed up in the sweetest way. Either healing someone, giving someone a prophetic word or for me to simply be pampered, God is definitely in the pampering business.

Cloaked Rebellion

Thus far, all of the stories you have read have been while I was living in the United States. However, I need to share one that transpired while living in South Korea. How I got to South Korea will be told in detail later on, but for now, I must share how delayed obedience to God is indeed cloaked rebellion.

Even though I lived about two hours from Seoul, I would travel to Seoul for church as well as to get my hair done. One day, after arriving at the hair salon, I encountered a very tall African man getting his hair cut. As I looked at the man, I felt like I needed to tell him about Jesus. But as I was waiting, and he was getting his hair cut, I was thinking of every reason that I should wait until he was done.

While he was still in the chair, I was taken to another part of the salon, and reasoned in my mind that I would tell him about Jesus, once I was done with my wash. But of course, once I sat up he was gone.

When I got back to the front of the salon, I asked the owner about the man and told the owner, who is not a Christian, that I needed to tell the man about Jesus. She laughed and said that he came into cut the very little hair he had on his head, every now and then. I said to the Lord, please forgive me and give me another opportunity.

Well, the following week a friend wanted to get her hair done, and wanted me to take her to the salon I frequented. Upon walking into the salon, there was the man. I went to the back of the shop with my friend and excitedly told her about what had happened the previous week. Once I told her everything, I left her to go talk to the man, but he had already left the shop.

The hairdresser said that he was an ambassador from South Africa, and they were really surprised to see him in the salon so soon after his last haircut. I felt the fear of the Lord because I realized that in my heart I did not have the 'boldness', I once had for immediately, saying what God told me to say.

It had been a little over six years since being saved, and having had spent two years in Korea, I realized at that point in time that I wasn't focused on hearing God for others, due to the fact that I wanted to get to where I needed to go, navigate through all of the demonic activity that was prevalent in the country, and then travel back home in order to lock myself in the comforts of my own home.

By the time I was dealing with the South African in the salon, I had already ministered in a number of churches in Korea as well as in other parts of South East Asia. In addition, my focus while in Korea was on the students in my classes, as well as the Koreans that God put on my path.

Had I fallen out of love with Jesus? Was that the reason for why I did not immediately speak to the ambassador the first time I saw him? Was it the fear of man, creeping back into my life, or was it simply hidden, and just manifesting itself again? Or simply, did I stop caring about the salvation of those I encountered? Whichever the reason, there I was, not sharing the love of God with someone who lived almost a 100 miles from me, that I have now seen, twice within a week.

Well God is so, patient, loving, merciful, and kind, because a few weeks later, I go back to the salon to get my hair done. As I am waiting to get my hair washed, the owner comes over to me, remembering my story from the 1st and 2nd encounter with the South African man. She says, "Do you remember the South African man you talked about twice?" Looking confused at the fact that she remembered, I responded, "Yes." As the hairdresser smiles really big, she pointed pass a number of ladies waiting in the salon and told me, "You see the woman over there, that's his wife!"

Needless to say, I jumped up and ran over to the lady and told her everything. I told her how God wanted me to talk to her husband about Jesus, and that I had missed two opportunities to talk about the Lord. How it grieved my heart to have missed the opportunity to talk to him about Jesus. And God in His goodness brought me back to Seoul, and the salon during the time she would be there as well.

We talked about God. I told her how God moved me to South Korea, and she shared that she and her husband were members of a delegation who would be in South Korea for a couple of years due to the trade relationship between South Korea and South Africa. In the end, God let me bless her as it relates to her salon services, and to let her know that He knows them in a special way.

There is a minister by the name of Bobby Connors who has had, and continues to have, some of the most amazing testimonies I have ever heard. One day while driving from Florida back to Georgia, I was listening to one of his messages.

I don't remember the title of the message. I don't even remember the context of the message, but there is one thing that he said that I have repeated, not only to others, but to myself. While he talked about obedience, he said, *"Halfhearted or delayed obedience is cloaked rebellion."* When I heard those words, I pulled over onto the shoulder of the highway, got of my car, and began to cry. I began to repent about the minutes, and even days of delay due to my attempt to reason my way out of what God was telling me to do. The interesting thing is, if God said go to a nation that was in conflict, that was 'easy'. But when He said to do something that appeared to be mediocre, like, buy a specific bottle of milk for someone, I would ask, "Is that me wanting to do that?"

We have to realize that when God gives us a directive to say or do something, there is always a reason bigger and greater than what we can see or even sometimes understand. The scary part of delayed obedience, is that it is very easy for some to simply reason their way out of following through with what God said.

Why would He tell you to give away all of the money in your bank account when you have bills to pay? Why would He tell you to go to an enemy's house and give them something. How about, knowing and even hearing people talk about you, and yet, He tells you to give them a specific amount of money. Or knowing that a leader is not managing church finances the way they are supposed to, and yet, He tells you to give them a five-figure offering. I have been in all of these situations and then some. God always got the glory. His glory manifest by either my receiving more than what was given, or it manifested by me having another level of revelation of His nature. We must understand that no matter what we do, truly believing that it is for the glory of God, will eventually always work out for our good.

You don't need my stories; all you have to do is read from Genesis to Revelation. Almost every book is laden with stories of a person, or groups of people who simply did not do what they were supposed to do. Despite seeing God's manifested presence, His miracles, and His provisions, people still rebelled.

I remember while reading a number of such accounts, I said out loud, "What is it going to take for the Israelites to get it?" Then in my heart, I heard, 'What is it going to take for 'you' to get it?' The scariest thing for me is to possibly live having ignored the whisper in my own heart, while easily pointing out disobedience in others.

Willingly Choosing Disobedience

There are times when God in His goodness will stop you in your path of disobeying Him. There are also times when He will allow you to continue on that path and reap the rewards of your disobedience. Then there are those times, when He will send someone after you, to keep you from going in a direction that will eventually harm you, physically, and most of the time, emotionally.

There is a story in the Bible about Balaam's donkey. Balaam was a sorcerer who was summoned by King Balak of the Moabites to curse the Israelites as Moses was leading them toward Canaan. Balak promised to pay Balaam for bringing evil upon the Hebrews.

During the night, God came to Balaam and told him not to curse the Israelites. Balaam eventually sent the king's messengers away. He did, however, go with a second set of Balak's messengers after being warned by God. While on the way, Balaam's donkey saw the angel of God standing in their path and brandishing a sword. The donkey turned off the path which resulted in a beating from Balaam.

The second time the animal saw the angel, she pressed against a wall, crushing Balaam's foot, which again resulted in a beating. The third time the donkey saw the angel, she laid down under Balaam who beat her severely with his staff. At that point, the Lord opened the donkey's mouth and it said to Balaam, "What have I done to you to make you beat me these three times?" (Numbers 22:28, NIV)

Even though the above is a good summary, you need to read each verse in order to fully understand how God will do everything in His power to not only keep you from walking into sin, which leads to destruction, but He will even get an animal to talk to you in order to get your attention.

So Balaam rose in the morning, saddled his donkey, and went with the princes of Moab. 22 Then God's anger was aroused because he went, and the Angel of the Lord took His stand in the way as an adversary against him. And he was riding on his donkey, and his two servants were with him.

23 Now the donkey saw the Angel of the Lord standing in the way with His drawn sword in His hand, and the donkey turned aside out of the way and went into the field. So Balaam struck the donkey to turn her back onto the road. 24 Then the Angel of the Lord stood in a narrow path between the vineyards, with a wall on this side and a wall on that side. 25 And when the donkey saw the Angel of the Lord, she pushed herself against the wall and crushed Balaam's foot against the wall; so he struck her again.

26 Then the Angel of the Lord went further, and stood in a narrow place where there was no way to turn either to the right hand or to the left. 27 And when the donkey saw the Angel of the Lord, she lay down under Balaam; so Balaam's anger was aroused, and he struck the donkey with his staff. 28 Then the Lord opened the mouth of the donkey, and she said to Balaam, "What have I done to you, that you have struck me these three times?" 29 And Balaam said to the donkey, "Because you have abused me. I wish there were a sword in my hand, for now I would kill you!" 30 So the donkey said to Balaam, "Am I not your donkey on which you have ridden, ever since I became yours, to this day? Was I ever disposed to do this to you?" And he said, "No."

31 Then the Lord opened Balaam's eyes, and he saw the Angel of the Lord standing in the way with His drawn sword in His hand; and he bowed his head and fell flat on his face. 32 And the Angel of the Lord said to him, "Why have you struck your donkey these three times? Behold, I have come out to stand against you, because your way is perverse before Me. 33 The donkey saw Me and turned aside from Me these three times. If she had not turned aside from Me, surely I would also have killed you by now, and let her live."

34 And Balaam said to the Angel of the Lord, "I have sinned, for I did not know You stood in the way against me. Now therefore, if it displeases You, I will turn back." 35 Then the Angel of the Lord said to Balaam, "Go with the men, but only the word that I speak to you, that you shall speak." So Balaam went with the princes of Balak. 40 Balak sacrificed cattle and sheep, and gave some to Balaam and the officials who were with him. 41 The next morning Balak took Balaam up to Bamoth Baal, and from there he could see the outskirts of the Israelite camp. (Numbers 22:21-41 New King James Version)

One might assume that God does not intervene when danger is ahead, or when plots are being planned in order to cause harm. However, we must understand that God does give visions and dreams to warn us of potential problems on the horizon.

There was a person, who I will call Moyra, who I had not only seen demonic attacks coming towards her from people in her church, but I also had a number of dreams about her being attacked by witches who 'she' called friends.

After sharing with Moyra, on various occasions, that most of the problems she was having were associated with the people that she had called "friends", I had gotten to the point where I gave her two fingers, which represents the peace sign. I was no longer going to be associated with her after the last encounter.

However, after 'I' made the decision to end the friendship, I had a dream. In the dream, Moyra was surrounded by three people and the three people looked at me with evil expressions indicating that they knew, that I was aware that they meant Moyra harm. After having the dream, I would have normally called Moyra and told her about the three people. But I was done with all of the warnings. I had no idea who two of the people were, but I did know that one of the individuals was someone Moyra had known since college.

Moyra knew that the college friends husband's family, was involved in ancestral worship and that the person, herself was not truly serving God. But nonetheless, Moyra did not want to dissolve the relationship despite the fact that she had regular nightmares that she knew was associated with this person.

The following day, I had an appointment in the area in which Moyra resided. I did not tell her that I was in the area and was simply going to go straight home after my appointment.

Immediately, after walking out of the building where I had my appointment, I clearly heard the Lord say, "Call Moyra!" I honestly said, "Lord, I really do not want to deal with Moyra right now." But it was as if it was an emergency. So, I obeyed and called.

Once she found out that I was in her area, she sounded excited and we agreed to meet at a nearby restaurant. As soon as she sat down, I could see the fear of the Lord in her eyes and I thought, 'okay, here we go'.

I began to share with her the dream I had and gave her details as to how I could see what the three people were planning. As I shared, she just looked wide-eyed. She then shared that she was on her way to meet up with one of the ladies who was going to be with the 2nd one I noticed in my dream. Then she was going to see the 3rd woman later in the evening. After the meeting, I already knew that it would be the last time I was going to see Moyra who I had known for over five years.

It was also one of the longest weekends that I have had in a long time, because I focused on asking God, please show me where I have disobeyed you, ignored someone you sent my way, or ignored signs that were directing me to go another way. I thanked Him for His mercy for those things that, because of the position of my heart, I did not want to see or hear. I also wept over His goodness for keeping me from getting on the path that I knowingly and unknowingly strayed onto.

You see, even though it pleases God when we obey Him, God doesn't get joy out of us obeying Him, or disobeying Him, we are His joy, fully and completely. However, when we do disobey, God doesn't sit back and say, "Go ahead and play in the street with oncoming cars." He actually does everything to get our attention to get us, 'back on track'.

However, I have learned that He has a place for us to be, and a time for us to arrive. If 'you' decide to take the long route, God doesn't leave you. Just keep in mind, that once you get off of His path, you are now on the path that the enemy has set for you. Unfortunately, most people will blame God for any mishap, while refusing to acknowledge the fact that they chose to receive the benefits of their sin, versus God's reward for their obedience.

Finding My Stride

Jesus Comforts His Disciples

1 *"Do not let your hearts be troubled. You believe in God; believe also in me. 2 My Father's house has many rooms; if that were not so, would I have told you that I am going there to prepare a place for you? 3 And if I go and prepare a place for you, I will come back and take you to be with me that you also may be where I am. 4 You know the way to the place where I am going."*

Jesus the Way to the Father

5 *Thomas said to him, "Lord, we don't know where you are going, so how can we know the way?" 6 Jesus answered, "I am the way and the truth and the life. No one comes to the Father except through me. 7 If you really know me, you will know my Father as well. From now on, you do know him and have seen him." 8 Philip said, "Lord, show us the Father and that will be enough for us." 9 Jesus answered: "Don't you know me, Philip, even after I have been among you such a long time? Anyone who has seen me has seen the Father. How can you say, 'Show us the Father'? 10 Don't you believe that I am in the Father, and that the Father is in me? The words I say to you I do not speak on my own authority. Rather, it is the Father, living in me, who is doing his work. 11 Believe me when I say that I am in the Father and the Father is in me; or at least believe on the evidence of the works themselves. 12 Very truly I tell you, whoever believes in me will do the works I have been doing, and they will do even greater things than these, because I am going to the Father. 13 And I will do whatever you ask in my name, so that the Father may be glorified in the Son. 14 You may ask me for anything in my name, and I will do it.*

Jesus Promises the Holy Spirit

15 *"If you love me, keep my commands. 16 And I will ask the Father, and he will give you another advocate to help you and be with you forever— 17 the Spirit of truth. The world cannot accept him, because it neither sees him nor knows him. But you know him, for he lives with you and will be in you. 18 I will not leave you as orphans; I will come to you. 19 Before long, the world will not see me anymore, but you will see me. Because I live, you also will live. 20 On that day you will realize that I am in my Father, and you are in me, and I am in you. 21 Whoever has my*

commands and keeps them is the one who loves me. The one who loves me will be loved by my Father, and I too will love them and show myself to them."

22 Then Judas (not Judas Iscariot) said, "But, Lord, why do you intend to show yourself to us and not to the world?" 23 Jesus replied, "Anyone who loves me will obey my teaching. My Father will love them, and we will come to them and make our home with them. 24 Anyone who does not love me will not obey my teaching. These words you hear are not my own; they belong to the Father who sent me. 25 "All this I have spoken while still with you. 26 But the Advocate, the Holy Spirit, whom the Father will send in my name, will teach you all things and will remind you of everything I have said to you. 27 Peace I leave with you; my peace I give you. I do not give to you as the world gives. Do not let your hearts be troubled and do not be afraid.

28 "You heard me say, 'I am going away and I am coming back to you.' If you loved me, you would be glad that I am going to the Father, for the Father is greater than I. 29 I have told you now before it happens, so that when it does happen you will believe. 30 I will not say much more to you, for the prince of this world is coming. He has no hold over me, 31 but he comes so that the world may learn that I love the Father and do exactly what my Father has commanded me. (John 14:1-31)

"Come now; let us leave.

Transitioning Higher

After being in Southern California for one year, I knew that God was directing me to move to Georgia. God told me the exact date to move. I was also told, "***If it does not fit into your car, you cannot take it with you!***" That meant the 45inch flat screen TV and surround sound entertainment system. All of which were shipped from New York when I first moved. I rarely turned the system on, so getting rid of it wasn't an issue. I simply prayed to find out who God wanted me to give it to.

In addition to the entertainment system, He also had me get rid of all of my books. I had books from my time in high school to when I got saved, and started buying books on Christianity. How did He tell me to get rid of the books? I had a dream of Jesus using one of His arms and swiping all of my books off of my bookshelves. As His arm touched the books, they wouldn't fall to the floor, they would simply disappear, leaving only a few books. Actually, about 10 books remained, my Bibles, and a few other books that I needed to give to other people.

I must admit that I had a lot of fear as I prepared to tell my Senior Vice President (SVP) that I needed to leave. I realized that moving from New York to California was easy because God told me step by step where to go, what to do and when to do it. But this move, or shall I say the transition was different. He did not tell me 'step-by-step', but it was as if He wanted to see, what I would do, and how I would do what He directed. It was at this point in time that I knew I was being shown, how much I learned… or did not learn.

Some people would call it a test, but it did not feel like a test. It felt similar to when my dad was teaching me to ride a bike, and he would run alongside me, without holding my bike seat. We started out with him making sure I understood that he was holding my seat. He showed me his hands, then had me sit on the bike, and assured me, that he was holding on very tightly to the seat. But, while he was teaching me to ride, eventually, he stopped holding the seat. I didn't know that he wasn't holding on, until I looked and noticed his hands next to his side as he ran alongside me. As soon as I saw his hands and realized that he wasn't holding onto the back of the bike seat, I would get scared and tilt over. But after a few more attempts, I was riding on my own, with him right next to me, and eventually, far behind me, *with his eyes still on me.*

One of the issues that contributed to the fear I was feeling about transitioning to Georgia was the fact that I could not understand why God would move me from California, where everything was starting to go so very well. Going well meant, I was due for a raise and a substantial bonus. I had a church to call home and I had developed relationships with other Christians who were okay with me interacting with God and the spirit realm the way I did.

I also realized that the fear was also due to the fact that when God moved me from NYC, He had a job for me to transition into. But with this move, there was no job, no directive to even look for one, and I had no idea where I needed to be in Georgia. But nevertheless, I proceeded with preparing the transition plan and prayed not for direction, but for peace in my mind and heart.

The process of getting rid of my things was not only refreshing, but it also reconfirmed what I was supposed to do and when I was supposed to leave. A lot of people wait and wait, to move when God gives them a directive, but if God tells you that you are going to be married, and you don't like cleaning your own apartment, then you need to make it a point to start liking to clean your apartment. If God tells you, either directly, or through a number of prophetic words, that you are going to be a best-selling author, then you need to start writing. Regardless of what it is, if He says you need to move to another state or another country, then you need to start preparing by either, getting rid of things, or learning the basics of the language of the country you will move to.

I had already had most of my things packed in a few boxes when a friend came to visit. While we were talking, she mentioned a book that she were thinking about buying. Well, you guessed it. The book she mentioned was one of the books Jesus did not wipe off the shelf. After God dealt with my books, it was onto my plasma TV.

There was a Latino superintendent that did odd jobs around the apartment complex. He was always very kind and we spoke every time we saw each other. God made it clear that I was to give him the plasma TV and entertainment system.

When I saw him, I explained to him that God wanted me to give him the system. He was of stunned and did not want to receive it. I explained to him that he must receive it, and that God was blessing him and his family. I also told him that I believe this was a prophetic act in that he and his family would be moving soon.

After arriving at his apartment building, I met his wife. Upon entering his very small two-room space, his wife started to cry and proclaimed that she was right. God had told her that they were moving soon. The fact that the TV, electronic equipment, and speakers were too big to fit into their apartment, this confirmed for her that they were indeed moving to a larger space.

I have learned that God will always give insight into what He is about to manifest in the earth realm. When we are quiet in our heart and mind to the things of this world, and focused on what God is saying about what is happening in this world and in heaven, we are sure to be at peace taking each step in obedience to God. While leaving their apartment, there was one thing that was still left for me to do, and that was to tell my SVP that I needed to leave.

I must be honest and say that I delayed telling my SVP that I needed to move to Georgia. As I was attempting to draft an email in order to make an appointment with him, I received an email from his secretary scheduling our raise and bonus meeting. Basically, I procrastinated so much that I was put in the position where instead of hearing about a raise and receiving a bonus, I was going to be resigning.

I will never forget the day I walked into my SVP's office and the look he had on his face. He looked so proud of himself for having a successful year and was beginning to tell me how well I had done during my first year. But before he could tell me about the raise and bonus, I stopped him and said "I know this will not make any sense to you, and I know you will not believe what I am about to say, but I have to move to Georgia." He looked at me, wide-eyed, with his face and neck turning a deep red; he wasn't blushing, it was anger. He asked "Why?"

After reiterating to him that he would not understand even if I explained everything to him, I proceeded to give him the transition plan that would allow someone to take over all of the duties that I was responsible for. I handed him the plan that was created and shared how very thankful I was for the opportunity to work with him.

He began to verbalize his anger and disappointment by noting "Do you know how much it cost to get you here!" As I realized that he was not only angry but disappointed, I finished sharing what I needed to and proceeded to leave out of his office.

As my hand touched the door knob, he stopped me with a, "Wait a minute, what about working remotely from Georgia?" EVERYTHING in me was doing back-flips and the Holy Ghost dance. I could not believe what I was hearing.

Eventually, we decided that I would fly to California twice a month and manage everything from Georgia. According to the SVP, I was also going to receive my raise and bonus due to the fact that I had earned them. I could not believe that I was prepared to walk away from what was going to be a six-figure salary and ended up not only receiving the salary, but I was moving to a state where my living expenses were going to be reduced by three times.

It did not take me long to rejoice in this scripture,

"Mark my words, no one who sacrifices house, brothers, sisters, mother, father, children, land—whatever—because of me and the Message will lose out. They'll get

it all back, but multiplied many times in homes, brothers, sisters, mothers, children, and land—but also in troubles. And then the bonus of eternal life! This is once again the Great Reversal: Many who are first will end up last, and the last first." (Mark 10:29-31 Message)

I realized that leaving California and the job wasn't about money. It was always about not having anything, or the desires of others, come before God in my heart. I realized that I did not want to disappoint the team I worked so well with, or the SVP who I had developed a good working relationship with. The environment was completely different from working in New York. Same type of business; banking and investments. But this team was like a family. Does this sound familiar?

There are so many ways that we can put others before God, knowingly and unknowingly. I knew that I was supposed to meet with my SVP, but I reasoned in my head that I would get everything in my apartment in order first, then tell him, last. But, yet again, God in His goodness, and His ever so abundant mercies had me address the issue way before I wanted to. However, after that meeting, everything seemed to take off at rapid speed.

I had prayed about which route I was supposed to take, but even more so, which city or town I needed to move to. While searching on the internet, I discovered an apartment complex in an area called Duluth. While speaking with the rental agent, I discovered that God had just moved her and her husband from California to Georgia a few weeks prior. They too were told to drive, and given such, they provided me with the directions they took in order to avoid traffic delays during the drive.

Yes, there were various maps that could give me directions, but there were a couple of options that I could take. I simply prayed and asked God to please tell me exactly which route He wanted me to take, and there He was, yet again, using this couple, who by the way, were children of pastors, to tell me which roads to take.

After realizing that everything God wanted me to do, and how He wanted me to do it was being laid out, I recognized that I was always at peace and woke up every morning bubbling excitement wondering which directive He was going to give next. There were issues and challenges during these transitions, but honestly, I cannot remember them all. Actually, even as I am typing this now, only two come to mind. This is because all of what God did outweighed any attention I gave the enemy during those challenging moments.

There was one incident that could have ended horribly but again, God got the glory. I had to move out of my apartment temporarily in order for management to redo the paint, carpet and some other things. To this day, I am not sure why, because the apartment looked fine. Well, on the day I had to move back into my duplex apartment, the Latino man who God had given the television too, along with some other friends, came by to help me move.

While the Latino man was trying to move the refrigerator upstairs, *ALONE*, he lost his grip and he along with the refrigerator went tumbling down the cement stairs. Everyone started screaming, as he stood up a little dazed, with blood flowing down his forehead. I screamed, "Why would you try to move the refrigerator by yourself!" But then I realized that everyone was quiet and staring at me. After I calmed down, I asked, "Why are you all staring at me?" The man, wide-eyed said in Spanish, "Because you are speaking in perfect Spanish!" I pretty much was speaking perfect Spanish. I honestly, did not hear myself, nor realized that I was speaking Spanish. But God wanted to let that man know that He was going to be speaking to him because He cared about everything associated with this man. This was the 2nd time God allowed me to speak in another language. The first time it was Chichewa, which I had never heard, nor studied. I had studied Spanish years prior, in high school and in Spain. But like those of you who have studied foreign languages, once you stop using it, you lose it...most of it.

Once I had everything in my car, I left California early in the morning, rejoicing and excited. I had the directions He had given me, and a CD changer filled with praise and worship CDs that would last me for the couple of days drive.

During my first day of driving, I noticed that there was a pickup truck that stayed close behind me. Being that there were not a lot of cars on the road, I simply moved to the next lane, but then I noticed that he moved to the next lane as well... and was closer than what is considered normal. Thankfully, we approached some other cars, and as I proceeded to stay behind a car, he came closer, and then as I went around a car, in order for him to be behind the other car, he dangerously cut in between me and the other car just to be behind me. Due to the fact that he was so close behind me, and then at a point in time, close to my right, I could see that he was truly demonic possessed. He was swaying back and forth in his seat as well as growling and glaring at me.

At the time I was driving a car that could go to 0-60 in 5.5secs, so I thought that this was a great opportunity to see how fast I could go, and away I went leaving him in the distance. But I also knew that I needed to pull off the highway once I reached an exit. Once I exited the highway, I was able to find a gas station that had other people. As I turned into the gas station, I realized that I was trembling from fear. I admit that I was scared and needed to pray off the fear that made me feel as though God wasn't with me, or God was setting me up for failure. However, I knew with everything in me, that I was on the right road, and heading where I needed to be. Why? Because the enemy manifested itself and it wasn't happy.

It took me some time to realize that when you are going in the direction that God has destined for you, opposition will indeed come. If opposition does not come you might want to ask yourself, if you are on God's path or the enemy's? If you are going in the direction that the enemy wants you to head, he will most likely cheer you on as you head into destruction.

For example, when I told people that I was going to Paris to party for the weekend, the response I received was "WOW, great, have a wonderful time." But when I told people that I was going to Africa or Asia for missions, it was "Why would you want to do that, you should help people in America..." Or even better, when I used to say, "Drinks are on me tonight..." while at a club, everyone would be excited. But then, when I shared that I had given money to help feed orphans, I was told, "You shouldn't give your money to those organizations...." Sometimes, the opposition that is tantamount to making you want to question God, is a clear indication that you are indeed heading in the right direction.

Once I reached Atlanta, I cannot explain how excited I was. In addition, I had only seen pictures of the apartment on the internet, so I was praying and believing that it would be located in a quiet area, and it indeed was.

While signing the lease agreement, I was asked if I wanted to sign a six-month or one-year term. As you know, with six-month leases, the rent is higher compared to a one year lease. I 'felt' as though I was supposed to sign a six-month lease. But I reasoned, yes, even at that point in my journey from California to Georgia, and knowing God is ALWAYS right, I reasoned with God saying that it did not make financial sense to sign a six month lease. So, I disobediently signed a one-year lease.

Again, for those who know about leases, if you sign a one year lease and you break the lease, meaning you move out of your apartment, you either have to pay a penalty, along with the remaining months until someone moves in, or just a very high penalty.

Long story short, I ended up signing a contract for my first home *SIX MONTHS* later. Yes...I know, I didn't listen. When I don't, or when 'you' don't listen, it always costs something. It may be time, money, or even a relationship, but when God calls us to do something, there is always a reason. We will know the reason, immediately, or later in life. However, in this situation, *Thank God* someone wanted to move into my apartment where I did not have to pay rent for the six months remaining on my lease.

Being obedient to Him is always for a purpose that He has established for us. It ties into a great blessing for us directly, for a friend, a family member, and a lot of times, a complete stranger. Whichever the reason, obeying Him isn't about getting something in the end. It is, and should always be about our hearts being so in love with Him, that we know that our obedience to His guidance is one of the ways we know, that He knows, we are displaying our love for Him, here on earth realm.

"If you love Me, you will keep My commandments. I will ask the Father, and He will give you another Helper, that He may be with you forever..." (John14:15-16 NIV)

The Message version puts it this way:

"If you love me, show it by doing what I've told you. I will talk to the Father, and he'll provide you another Friend so that you will always have someone with you. This Friend is the Spirit of Truth. The godless world can't take him in because it doesn't have eyes to see him, doesn't know what to look for. But you know him already because he has been staying with you, and will even be in you!" (John 14:15-17 Message)

Remaining in His love, isn't just about selfishly benefiting from being loved by God. We need to understand that by joining in on His love for others is what He requires of everyone who has received His love.

It's all about focusing on others, or 'focusing out' is something that I often tell people when they ask about seeing and hearing spiritually. Most people are seeking to hear God or see visions for 'themselves'. They are not concerned with being a blessing, or being *the* blessing for other people.

Most people that I have met, from around the world, who are seers, tend to have the same stories concerning how God will show them what someone else needed to know. However, we can prophesy, have visions of people's past, present and future, and then for some reason, turn around and trip over something, or fall into a ditch that we could not see for ourselves.

I think this happens for two reasons. One, it is that God does not want those who are very sensitive to the spirit realm, may it be seers, prophets, (those in the office, or prophesy is their strongest gift) to walk alone believing that they do not need anyone else. We all need other people in the body of Christ to walk along side of, but unfortunately, I have seen way too often, people wanting a person living, *in* the gifts of the prophetic, healing, etc, to simply give them a word, but never want to be the giver of a word. In other words, people most often want to use individuals who are walking in their gifts, versus giving to those who are gifted. When I say give, I am not only referring to money or resources, but prayer, intercession, or simply friendship without any hidden motives. I once heard a pastor say, "I had to learn a long time ago that you give people your gifts, but you don't give them you. Everyone should be blessed by your gifts, but God will select a few to walk with you, who you will be accountable to and will simply be your friend." Given the fact that so many people are used for their gifts, in the beginning of their walk, they develop a "I don't need anyone stance." Which is a sure way for them to walk uncovered, or alone, and eventually fall into a ditch that they might not be able to get out of. Walking with others allows you to not only have needed fellowship, but it also brings people into your life who will love you in a way that allows you to grow in your gift, as well as in integrity and honor. The challenge is determine who is in your life for your gift, versus those who are in your life because they truly love you. It does take time to figure this out, but once you do, you will find that you are walking with a community of believers who will not only pray with you way into the night, but will travel to the other side of the world to simply sit with you.

The second reason I believe that those who walk in a strong gift of prophecy can sometimes see more for others than for themselves is that God wants to make sure that pride does not become an issue. For example, I have met many people who refuse to listen to correction, take advice, or be mentored. I have also seen these individuals question those who really are concerned about how they use their gift. These gifted individuals may be known around the world, or in their church for their prophetic and healing gifts. But when there are no seminars, conferences, church services, or group activities where their gifts are on display, they do not say, 'Hi', 'Good Morning', or simply acknowledge someone else who doesn't have an impressive title.

They do not understand that 'being nice' is more important than being able to prophecy. When God brings individuals around them to help them see that they are 'not' their gift, but they are created to exist in the image of Christ, which is to first, love those you encounter, they may find themselves falling into a ditch, until they come to realize that they really do need wise counsel. These wise counselors are a set of individuals who consist of a core group of either, family, friends, and mentors who are not impressed with their gift(s).

I will always be thankful for individuals that God has brought into my life, starting two years into my walk with Him who were able to correct, not only my actions, but point out the motives of my heart. I have since learned that if God has to bring people into your life, to 'consistently' correct you, then you have ignored the one who is the ultimate corrector that this is the Holy Spirit.

God has had me walk up to people, individuals that I have known for some time and some I had just met, in order to share something with them that they simply did not want to hear. I must admit, once I heard it, I would do two things, start to sweat and say to God, "If they are not listening to you, why would they listen to me…besides, they are going be angry at me?" I never got an answer to that question. But I must share that most people do not get angry. However, those who do become offended or angry, normally find a way to get in contact with me and share how they 'were' angry but I was right. I make sure that I tell them, "I wasn't trying to be right because I wasn't trying to be in your personal business." They normally start to laugh and then share how the word they received changed their life.

When I began my walk with the Lord, individuals, mostly well-season women in the Lord would point out something in me that was wrong. My first response was, 'Nooooo not I'. But, within 24 hours or less, God would give me a vision or a dream not only confirming their word(s), but also showing me different events associated with what I was told. After each realization, I would have to repent to God and apologize to the person I sinned against. The sin was being *offended.*

It's unfortunate, but most people repent to God, but never go to the person that they sinned against. One must realize that true repentance requires you to not only 'stop' what you were doing, but also say 'sorry' to the person you did it to. I remember a preacher saying, "I can tell how anointed you are, by how quick you say sorry."

The Way of Love

1 If I speak with human eloquence and angelic ecstasy but don't love, I'm nothing but the creaking of a rusty gate. 2 If I speak God's Word with power, revealing all his mysteries and making everything plain as day, and if I have faith that says to a mountain, "Jump," and it jumps, but I don't love, I'm nothing.

3-7 If I give everything I own to the poor and even go to the stake to be burned as a martyr, but I don't love, I've gotten nowhere. So, no matter what I say, what I believe, and what I do, I'm bankrupt without love.

> *Love never gives up.*
>
> *Love cares more for others than for self.*
>
> *Love doesn't want what it doesn't have.*
>
> *Love doesn't strut,*
>
> *Doesn't have a swelled head,*
>
> *Doesn't force itself on others,*
>
> *Isn't always "me first,"*
>
> *Doesn't fly off the handle,*
>
> *Doesn't keep score of the sins of others,*
>
> *Doesn't revel when others grovel,*
>
> *Takes pleasure in the flowering of truth,*
>
> *Puts up with anything,*
>
> *Trusts God always,*
>
> *Always looks for the best,*
>
> *Never looks back,*
>
> *But keeps going to the end.*

8-10 Love never dies. Inspired speech will be over some day; praying in tongues will end; understanding will reach its limit. We know only a portion of the truth, and what we say about God is always incomplete. But when the Complete arrives, our incompletes will be canceled.

11 When I was an infant at my mother's breast, I gurgled and cooed like any infant. When I grew up, I left those infant ways for good. 12 We don't yet see things clearly. We're squinting in a fog, peering through a mist. But it won't be long before the weather clears and the sun shines bright! We'll see it all then, see it all as clearly as God sees us, knowing him directly just as he knows us!

13 But for right now, until that completeness, we have three things to do to lead us toward that consummation: Trust steadily in God, hope unswervingly, love extravagantly. And the best of the three is love. (1 Corinthians 13) The Message

Church Location

Once I settled into my new apartment in Georgia, I started to search for a church. I had a friend, Angelique, who came to visit during my 2nd week in Georgia. We had already decided to visit a church that was a 45-minute drive from where I lived. Actually, "I" had already decided that this particular church was going to be my home church until God changed that.

I had a dream about a minister that I had seen minister via internet broadcast, as well as on Christian television. I had heard a lot about the person's ministry being in another state and all they were doing as it relates to prayer and the prophetic. In the dream, I saw this minister praying for nations.

I woke up and googled the location of the church and found out that they had just established a church, 15 minutes from my apartment and was holding 5 am prayer. I woke Angelique and asked if it was okay to attend the church. She was excited to visit the church as well.

Upon reaching the church, around 4:30 am, we had to stand on the line that had what looked like a little over a hundred men and women waiting to get in and join in prayer. I was excited and so elated that God not only did it again as it related to guiding me to the place He wanted me to be, but it was only 15 minutes away from where I was living.

While in the church, I was so elated to be around people who clearly enjoyed prayer. But at the same time, I realized that my ears were buzzing with a piercing sound that also let me know that there was a lot of other things going on in the church that required not only more prayer, but that the enemy was coming against those who were seeking to 'hear' the Lord.

Here is a little inside information, buzzing in your ears, outside of a medical issue of tinnitus, represents a demonic interference in the environment... coming from 'inside' the environment. Most of the time I have found that it comes from those who complain, backbite and gossip. The Bible clearly says that sweet and bitterness should not come from the same tongue. However, most people don't realize that as they retain relationships with people who gossip, or constantly complain, they are not only empowering the demonic realm around them, but giving the enemy authority to wreck havoc on their life and those around them. The more you complain and gossip in order to speak ill of people, the less you hear God and the more you entertain the enemy's voice.

Taming the Tongue

Not many of you should become teachers, my fellow believers, because you know that we who teach will be judged more strictly. 2 We all stumble in many ways. Anyone who is never at fault in what they say is perfect, able to keep their whole body in check. 3 When we put bits into the mouths of horses to make them obey us, we can turn the whole animal. 4 Or take ships as an example. Although they are so large and are driven by strong winds, they are steered by a very small rudder wherever the pilot wants to go. 5 Likewise, the tongue is a small part of the body, but it makes great boasts. Consider what a great forest is set on fire by a small spark. 6 The tongue also is a fire, a world of evil among the parts of the body. It corrupts the whole body, sets the whole course of one's life on fire, and is itself set on fire by hell.

7 All kinds of animals, birds, reptiles and sea creatures are being tamed and have been tamed by mankind, 8 but no human being can tame the tongue. It is a restless evil, full of deadly poison. 9 With the tongue we praise our Lord and Father, and with it we curse human beings, who have been made in God's likeness. 10 Out of the same mouth come praise and cursing. My brothers and sisters, this should not be. 11 Can both fresh water and salt water flow from the same spring? 12 My brothers and sisters, can a fig tree bear olives, or a grapevine bear figs? Neither can a salt spring produce fresh water. (James 3:1-12)

At a specific point in time, as the minister spoke, I couldn't hear anything other than the piercing buzz, but I knew, even with the uncomfortable buzzing, I would be joining the church.

God guiding me to this specific church was quite a different experience from when I was in California and God told me to attend a church that was over an hour away. Actually, Angelique, who was visiting me in Georgia, was the one who told me about two different churches that I should visit once I had moved to Los Angeles. After researching information about both churches online, I prayed for God to let me know which of them He wanted me to attend. So, the night prior to church, I printed out directions for both of the churches, but I did not pull out the printed directions until Sunday morning.

Once I woke up, I went up to my den area to see the directions for each church. The church that I had printed first, those pages were blank, and the church that I had printed 2nd, those pages were very clear. Now, I know what you are thinking, that the printer simply ran out of ink. However, if it did run out of ink, then the first church's address should have printed and the 2nd one should have been blank. So, I knew that I was going to be taking the hour drive to church.

When I reached the church and service began, every word that the pastor spoke hit me right in my heart and mind. I was crying and snotting during the entire service. I felt as though God had a hold of this man's tongue and was not only reminding me of all the things He had done in my past, but He was letting me know that He brought me to Los Angeles. He brought me to this particular church, and the plans that He had for me were plans that I could never imagine. I was excited and expectant of what He was about to reveal. I knew that God was making firm my steps because I not only thoroughly enjoyed hearing someone pontificate on the scriptures like I had never heard before, but I also was surrounded by people who also delved deep into the word and loved it.

The LORD makes firm the steps of the one who delights in him;
(Psalm 37:23)

While driving home from each of those church services, the one in California and the one in Georgia, I was so thankful that God knew what I needed at those specific points in my life. I needed to be steeped in His word while in California and develop a prayer life while in Georgia. I did not realize that later on He would lead me to a church where I could put everything that I had learned together, the word, prayer, and my encounters with angels and demons so that I could be sent to the nations. But He knew what He was doing, and I must admit that I was enjoying each step I obediently took *in* Him and *towards* Him.

Many are the plans in a person's heart, but it is the LORD's purpose that prevails. (Proverbs 19:21)

Convergence in the 24hr Prayer Center

As I had previous mentioned, immediately after being saved, God placed me in a church, in Los Angles that was focused on the Word. At that time, it was exactly what I needed. Please note that we should 'always' be focused on the Word, however, when one is newly saved, I have realized that God takes us all through a process, step-by-step, specific to our individual make-up and according to what He desires, from us and with us.

At the time, I had so many questions as to how things were tied together in the Old Testament and New Testament. I wanted to know why there were four gospels, and not just one. Why did we have to have Kings and Chronicles which basically repeats the same stories? What was it about the apostles that Jesus saw, that God saw that made Jesus choose them? Why did God make the earth, round and not like an octagon? Why did we need the blood of Jesus and not simply water? Are we saved because we acknowledge God with the faith He gave us, or is it our free-will to choose Him and that is why we are saved? And, if that is the case, how does our free-will and His faith work in tandem with each other so that we can live this glorious life in Him? So many questions! The more answers I got, the more questions I had.

During my time in California, I did learn how to study the word, walk in miracles, heed His voice, but it was my first year in Georgia, where I learned how to pray. I mean really pray. I did not know that I did not know how to strategically pray until I heard someone teach on prayer.

The church in California prayed and taught about praying to God, but there was a whole other dimension when it came to praying, interceding and wailing. Nevertheless, God told me to serve at the prayer center and I was like, "Eh?" I was to serve the hours that were the hardest to fill, from 12:00 am to 6:00 am, a.k.a, the bewitching hours. I never knew why they were called the bewitching hours, but I found out quickly.

It was between the hours of 12 am – 3 am that most cults and witches would call Christian prayer lines and attempt to curse those who were answering the calls. Those stories are for another book, at another time, but the one that fits the purpose of this book is the one where God told me to "Drive slow!" when I was concerned about driving on icy roads.

After working at the prayer center for a few weeks, I was in a car accident. Someone ran a red light and slammed into the driver-side of my car. I had issues with my left hand, as well as twitches in my right arm due to muscle and nerve damage.

I had taken off from the prayer center in order to recoup, but the Lord woke me up and told me to go serve at the prayer center. I reluctantly, and with a bad attitude got up and dressed. As soon as I stepped foot onto the pavement outside, I slipped but did not fall. The pavement was covered with black ice.

I complained, "God, it's black ice out here, don't you care that I might be in another accident?" I heard as clear as day "**Drive Slow?**" I actually giggled and got into my car and slowly drove to the prayer center.

Upon reaching the prayer center, 95% if not more, of the calls were from people who were in car accidents and had pain. EVERYONE I prayed for, was healed. Praise the Lord, 'right'! Well, my attitude had to adjust to the fact that I was sitting there in pain as I prayed for others.

After the first few calls, I realized what God was doing. He was showing me my heart towards, not those He was healing, but towards Him who I was blaming for the accident. He also showed me that I was believing that He was loving those He healed, more than He loved me. I know that is not the case, but at that point in time, if He did not allow me to realize that I was believing and empowering a lie, I would have had no idea of the accusations I had *against* God in my heart.

We can accuse God of so many things where in actuality, it is either the enemy trying to get us to believe a lie that suits his purpose. In addition, it could be something that is unknowingly planted in our heart, that remains unseen until the Holy Spirit reveals it to us. Most of the time people say it doesn't matter if it's your flesh, or the devil, we just want God to get rid of it.

God wants His people to know that He loves them and that He is not a God who is out to get them. However, when we walk from under God's love covering and walk in our own way, it gives an opening for the enemy to activate his plans in our life. Especially when things are appearing to go a little haywire at work, with family, or even at the supermarket, I always do a spirit, heart, and surroundings check. I ask God to show me any issues in my heart that I am not aware of by praying, "God search my heart so that you can show me what's in it."

When we give our heart to God, it is only then will we truly know what's in it and what needs to be changed. If He does not have our heart, if we have not fully surrendered to Him, then we could be at times, unknowingly serving two masters; God and whatever, or whomever else we have exalted in our mind and heart.

A surrounding check also involves asking Him to show me who is in my life that He has assigned to it, or is there someone in my life on assignment from the enemy. I remember sharing that one should never go into covenant with someone who has 'an unstable' mind. Yet, even though I shared that, I found that there were a number of people that I was in covenant with, but they were not in covenant with God, even though they *pretended* to be.

I had to learn, and unfortunately, had a few lessons of being with people who, one minute they believe in God, and the next minute they did not. They were always going through deliverance from demonic forces, for things they did not want to let go of, and gave a plethora of excuses as to why they had a right to be, angry, bitter, jealous, and unforgiving.

In the beginning of my walk with God, I was very quick to walk away from these type of people. But God had allowed me to be in a number of situations in order to, not only understand His grace and mercy that He had for them, but His grace and mercy He had for me as well.

I would find myself praying, "God tell me if this is 'my' assignment or not." Until He told me to walk away, I would stay and pray until He said otherwise. However, I have seen so many people, who simply won't listen to God. Actually, it is more of an issue of choosing Him over money, drugs, food, and most of the time family.

Someone once said that when a person won't receive correction, there's not much one can do to help them. When you find that people make excuses for their ungodly behavior--or blame others--rather than seeking the Lord's grace to change, all one can do is pray and release them to their own devices. *I've learned the hard way not to counsel demons, or walk around the seemingly eternal mountain with people who refuse to listen to godly wisdom. If people will not listen, all you can do is pray.*

By serving at the prayer center, I could see how praying the Word not only is one of the most perfect ways to pray for other people, it is the main way one should pray to keep themselves covered and protected, naturally and spiritually.

I remember being in a hotel room with three people after a conference. We were sharing the same room, and after we all went to sleep, demons began to fly into the room. Yes, you read that correctly, demons came into the room. They bypassed me and began to attack the people in the room.

While this was happening, I was sleeping, and the next morning upon waking up, they asked me, how I could sleep through what was transpiring in the room. They said that at some point, in the middle of the night, we all popped up and they asked me if something just flew into the room. I answered "Yes", and went right back to sleep.

They were angry at the fact that I was not getting attacked and they were. As I got out of bed, I looked at them both and told them that the reason they were being attacked was because they were angry and bitter, amongst other things. All of which opens us all up to a demonic onslaught of things.

I realized how the position of our heart not only puts us in a position where we disobey God, but we actually simply start obeying the enemy. If we don't continuously walk out His plans, then we are walking out the enemies plans. But there are so many people who believe that they are protected by God because they pray for His protection. The only issue is, they don't want anything else from God outside of what He provides.

While serving in the prayer center, I also realized that there were so many people praying, what I remember one minister, called 'anemic prayers'. Prayers that are considered powerless, not because they lacked eloquence, but because they do not know Him. Their prayers are proceeding from first, unclean lips, and from a heart that does not believe that God is out to love them, but to 'get' them.

When you think about it, the human heart is quick to accuse God of all that is wrong, not realizing that God simply wants us to realize that He is for us, and not against us. The subtle accusations that are in anyone's heart greatly impacts their prayer lives, and puts them in a position, where they are going through the motions of praying, but have no peace, or power in the process.

Until we understand His passion for us, we offer up weak words that express our desperate wish for him to listen, versus standing boldly before His throne of grace, and giving him praise for who He is... knowing that He hears all of our petitions.

13. These things I have written to you who believe in the name of the Son of God, so that you may know that you have eternal life. 14This is the confidence which we have before Him, that, if we ask anything according to His will, He hears us. 15And if we know that He hears us in whatever we ask, we know that we have the requests which we have asked from Him....(1 John 5:13-15)

No Job, No Money, But God!

I had been working, either a part-time job, a full-time job, or both since I was 14 years old. I did not know what it was like not to have a job, or a steady income.

Once I returned to the United States from earning my MBA in England, I was offered jobs where management did not want to pay me what my counterparts, who were opposite in every way from me, were being paid. How did I respond to this? I started my own company. However, once I got saved, I did not want to work, I wanted to either leave the country to help feed the poor and hold orphan babies, or just spend hours reading my Bible and worshiping God.

In 2008, God answered a prayer I had been praying for two years, He pulled me off of my job. No more 60 hours a week, adrenaline rushing activities. No longer would I have to fly across the country or deal with the various issues of being in the financial industry. I was in a state of euphoria for about 48 hours. Then, panic struck… I had neither a job nor a steady income. I did not know that I was about to embark on, yet, I was at the beginning of another journey that was going to take me places that I could not have imagined.

Prior to 2008, Wall Street had already started to rumble with issues that some of us knew were going to end badly. People who do not work in the financial arena fail to realize that there are thousands of people who could speculate, as well as calculate, potential trouble on the horizon.

There were those who used the storms for their advantage, and there were some who simply did not prepare.[23] There was no such thing as 'unforeseen, unanticipated, unexpected, or sudden' events on Wall Street. There are always those who know what is going. And for Christians, there are those of us who can feel, and hear God when it relates to things that are about to shift.

It was November 2007 when God woke me up and told me to transfer money from one investment account to another. In addition, He also told me to move all of my money to a different financial firm. I won't go into the details of all of the financial talk, but what I will share is, no matter how smart, or educated you are... in any field... GOD KNOWS MORE...because He is all knowing.

It was a Wednesday morning when I called my broker and informed him of the transactions that I wanted executed. He informed me that it wasn't a wise move and that I should speak with his supervisor, in order for the supervisor to restate what the broker had already said. I simply refused their advice and they proceeded to send me the necessary forms to close out the accounts, as well as transfer a substantial amount of money to a new firm. It normally takes 24-48 hours to close out/transfer various investments. By Friday, all the documents had been processed.

---

[23]In 2009, the number of U.S. households with a net worth of $1 million or more, excluding wealth derived from a primary residence increased by 16 percent according to the Spectrem Group, a Chicago-based consulting firm. After a 27 percent decline in the number of millionaire households in 2008, the ranks of U.S. millionaires swelled to 7.8 million last year. And, for the "*Ultra High Net Worth Individual*," defined as someone with a net worth of $5 million or more, that population grew 17 percent in 2009 to 980,000. In addition, according to the Global Wealth of 2013, issues by the Boston Consulting Group (BCG), private financial assets worldwide reached $135.5-trillion in 2012 – a 7.8% increase from the prior year and a marked recovery from the tepid 3.6% growth in 2011. This contributed to the number of the world's millionaires rising by 50% between 2008 and 2013.
.

Monday morning, I arrived at my office, and everyone was in an uproar, or shall I say panic. After settling in, I asked my administrators what was happening. They said that the bank we were working for had issued a 'blackout period' on all accounts and the fund holding our 401ks was tanking, along with other accounts they managed.

I know that I wrote that I would not get into all of the financial jargon, but you have to understand the meaning of a 'blackout period'. A blackout period is a period of at least three consecutive business days, but not more than 60 days during which the majority of employees at a particular company, are not allowed to make alterations to their retirement or investment plans. A blackout period usually occurs when major changes are being made to a financial strategy for a corporation. In a firm, a blackout period may happen because a plan is being restructured or altered, for example, if a pension fund is shifting from one fund manager to another at a different bank. It is also called a 'lock-down'.

What I did not know at the time, was that in July, earlier that year, the company I was working with was seized by federal regulators. The company's capital was being lost due to downgrades in their rating, associated with the poor quality of their accounting books that were being revealed. Within days of the downgrades, depositors pulled out approximately 7.5% of the bank's deposits. And given the plethora of issues within the industry, uninsured depositors, lost an estimated $270 million.

Given that I had already moved all of my investments to another company, I was not affected by the blackout period, and my financial analyst and clerical staff could see it on my face.

"God told you to do something didn't He?" This was asked by a co-worker who was of another faith. I said, "He sure did!" I explained what had happened Wednesday morning. They asked why didn't I inform them of what was about to happen. I responded, *"Why...so you can pimp Jesus? I don't think so!"*

I realized then, that some things were about to change, but I wasn't sure what. A few weeks later, the company laid off close to 300 people. Then, at the beginning of December, it laid off another few hundred.

By the time January 2008 rolled around, one person from my staff was cut and I knew more cuts were coming. When I received a call, noting that my department was no longer needed, I was ready. In actuality, I consoled the person who called me to tell me that I no longer needed to fly back to California.

Upon hanging up the phone, I jumped up and down, praised God and then it hit me, my car note, mortgage payment, student loans, and credit card bills… and NO JOB! Let the fun begin.

During this world-wide tumultuous time, Psalm 37 and 73 kept coming to my mind. Both of these passages of scriptures give Christians guidance on not envying the wicked when they prosper.

The fundamental question underlying Psalm 73 is, "How can a good God allow the righteous to suffer?" This question has puzzled me, as well as other Christians, and at the same time, pleased skeptics, of which I was one, prior to loving Jesus. This psalm and the questions with which it deals are extremely important. You should do a study on both Psalms. But for the purpose of this book, I will tell you this.

After all the required documents and conference calls were executed, I was officially no longer working. During the transition out from the company, everyone was told that they would not receive a bonus due to the financial issues that the company faced. You know what I am about to say next, don't you? About a month after having my last interaction with the company, I was contacted by someone who stated that, 'someone' at the company said, "Make sure that Beverlin receives her bonus!"

What was my job at the company? I was responsible for making sure that everything, under the responsibility of my direct manager, was done with integrity and met all of the financial regulator's requirements.

A David Psalm 37 (The Message Version)

1-2 Don't bother your head with braggarts or wish you could succeed like the wicked. In no time they'll shrivel like grass clippings and wilt like cut flowers in the sun. 3-4 Get insurance with God and do a good deed, settle down and stick to your last. Keep company with God, get in on the best.

5-6 Open up before God, keep nothing back; he'll do whatever needs to be done: He'll validate your life in the clear light of day and stamp you with approval at high noon. 7 Quiet down before God, be prayerful before him. Don't bother with those who climb the ladder, who elbow their way to the top.

8-9 Bridle your anger, trash your wrath, cool your pipes—it only makes things worse. Before long the crooks will be bankrupt; God-investors will soon own the store. 10-11 Before you know it, the wicked will have had it; you'll stare at his once famous place and—nothing! Down-to-earth people will move in and take over, relishing a huge bonanza.

12-13 Bad guys have it in for the good guys, obsessed with doing them in. But God isn't losing any sleep; to him they're a joke with no punch line. 14-15 Bullies brandish their swords, pull back on their bows with a flourish. They're out to beat up on the harmless, or mug that nice man out walking his dog. A banana peel lands them flat on their faces—slapstick figures in a moral circus.

16-17 Less is more and more is less. One righteous will outclass fifty wicked, For the wicked are moral weaklings but the righteous are God-strong. 18-19 God keeps track of the decent folk; what they do won't soon be forgotten. In hard times, they'll hold their heads high; when the shelves are bare, they'll be full.

Financial Obedience:

$10,000 and $0.25 Are the Same

We can't talk about obedience, unless we discuss the one thing that God indicates is an option for you to serve… mammon.

No one can serve two masters; for either he will hate the one and love the other, or he will be devoted to one and despise the other. You cannot serve God and mammon. (Matthew 6:24)

During my walk with God, I have noticed four main causes for demonization, confusion, lack, setback, and a host of other issues in a *Christian's* life. They are unforgiveness, bitterness, jealousy, and the love of money.

I discussed unforgiveness earlier by asking how can we expect to receive God's forgiveness and yet, do not want to offer it to someone else. It is clear that if you have unforgiveness in your heart and you are refusing to forgive someone for the things they have said or done, then you are dealing with one of two things, self-righteousness, and/or you might not be saved. I know the 'might not be saved' part sounds harsh, but let's deal with the reality of each.

Many people ruin their lives by consuming a poison that only kills themselves, and that is anger, bitterness, jealousy and unforgiveness. Matthew 18 talks about being turned over to tortures if we don't forgive.

The Parable of the Unmerciful Servant

21 Then Peter came to Jesus and asked, "Lord, how many times shall I forgive my brother or sister who sins against me? Up to seven times?" 22 Jesus answered, "I tell you, not seven times, but seventy-seven times. 23 "Therefore, the kingdom of heaven is like a king who wanted to settle accounts with his servants. 24 As he began the settlement, a man who owed him ten thousand bags of gold was brought to him. 25 Since he was not able to pay, the master ordered that he and his wife and his children and all that he had be sold to repay the debt.

26 "At this the servant fell on his knees before him. 'Be patient with me,' he begged, 'and I will pay back everything.' 27 The servant's master took pity on him, canceled the debt and let him go. 28 "But when that servant went out, he found one of his fellow servants who owed him a hundred silver coins. He grabbed him and began to choke him. 'Pay back what you owe me!' he demanded.

29 "His fellow servant fell to his knees and begged him, 'Be patient with me, and I will pay it back.' 30 "But he refused. Instead, he went off and had the man thrown into prison until he could pay the debt. 31 When the other servants saw what had happened, they were outraged and went and told their master everything that had happened.

32 "Then the master called the servant in. 'You wicked servant,' he said, 'I canceled all that debt of yours because you begged me to. 33 Shouldn't you have had mercy on your fellow servant just as I had on you?'

*34 In anger his master handed him over to the jailers to be tortured, until he should pay back all he owed. 35 "**This is how my heavenly Father will treat each of you unless you forgive your brother or sister from your heart.**"*

*For if you forgive other people when they sin against you, your heavenly Father will also forgive you. But if you do not forgive others their sins, your Father will not forgive your sins. (*Matthew 6:14-15)

There are so many scriptures that show how much we are forgiven by God because of His mercy. There are also hundreds, if not thousands of books on teaching people the importance of forgiveness; both Christian and non-Christian. And yet, this is one of the main issues people still either ignore or refuse to contend with. Why? Why is unforgiveness still so prevalent?

People who profess to be Christians refuse to fully surrender their emotions to God! And even scarier, they believe that their judgment of the person is better than God's judgment. They believe that they have a right to hold unforgiveness, which in reality is anger and bitterness towards the person. Not realizing that their anger toward a person is their form of issuing judgment against a person...which basically kicks God out the position of judge.

Does this mean that you become best friends with a rapist or the thief who violated you, or even violated a friend or family member? Of course not! But what it does mean, is that as time passes, and you release all of the pain and hurt you experienced, God will use those traumatic experiences for His glory. What does that look like? You using your testimony to contribute to the healing of someone else who might have suffered the same thing.

The other issue is associated with money. The original Greek word for money is mammon. Mammon is the Greek form of an Aramaic word for "riches". In general, it was used as a personification of richness as an evil spirit. Upon researching the topic, it appears that mammon is the name of an evil spirit (personal or impersonal) with great power, specializing in greed and covetousness. It is in all actuality a spirit of financial dissatisfaction, in all certainty, a denial of God truly being Jehovah Jireh, our provider.

Before you continue to read, I must say that the following testimonies might offend some. Especially those who do not believe in giving, those who are cheap, and those who have allowed the spirit of religion and mammon to warp their minds to a point where they will never believe that God can, and always will, supernaturally provide provision for His children.

These testimonies are mine and are very real. They are similar to hundreds of others I have met all over the world who simply trust God for everything they have and have faith for resources to take the gospel around the world to help feed, house, and care for thousands.

If you are one of these people, who might feel offended, God bless you and be delivered in Jesus name.

Like with forgiveness, there are thousands of books as well as sermons that discuss how to overcome the spirit of mammon. But when you really acknowledge the fact that one has made money their God, knowingly or unknowing, the key to overcoming the spirit of mammon is being filled by a greater, more powerful Spirit, the Holy Spirit. And, renewing your mind as it relates to how money works in and for God's kingdom.

We must all understand that we are first required to use money in order to do what God requires of us, for our family and for others. But when we seek after money in order to be God for our family and others, then that is where the problem begins.

God showed me early in my walk how I had a spirit of mammon due to my focus on making as much money as I could. Being that I grew up very poor, my focus from the time I was in the seventh grade was to become one of the richest people in the world. I remember the day I said it, and the resolve in my heart that I was going to die knowing that I was wealthy. But after being saved, I knew nothing was ever going to be more important to me than Jesus Christ, including money. He was the one who talked to me about tithes a few months after being saved, and yet, the deep issues I had with the spirit/mindset of mammon wasn't made known to me until four years into being saved.

After being saved, I didn't have a problem with giving money to people God led me to. From $100 to thousands, it wasn't a problem until He pulled me off my job. I realized that it was easy to obey God when he said to give when I had the safety of credit cards, a six-figure income, and a substantial amount of money in investment and retirement accounts. But I remember the exact moment that I was delivered from a spirit of mammon.

You see, the spirit of mammon is in rebellion against God. Rebellion due to the fact that you are putting your trust in an inanimate object that is used as an exchange for goods and services. You can also look at it this way, when you read the scripture about mammon, Jesus did not say you couldn't serve God and money as He would not have said you cannot serve God and soap. Rather He said, you cannot serve the Almighty God and the Almighty Dollar. If being rich, or money itself were evil, God would command all of us to a life of poverty. Not to engage in dealing with money, and use other means of exchange for goods and services.

For me, realizing that I had trusted my job(s) for money, in order to give, provide for my family, as well as travel to where God desired for me to go, put me in a precarious predicament. I had to learn that He was indeed the provider, it wasn't the amount of work I did or the number of clients I had. It was He who gave me the wealth that I had accumulated. It was His favor on my life that opened doors for me and He was the one who put me in various positions to not only earn money but protect the money I had from the various market issues that were taking the financial world into a tailspin.

I can share stories of how God woke me up at night, told me to go to a certain location, and give someone a specific amount of money, right down to the penny. But there are three stories I would like to share. Each has to do with obeying His voice as it relates to giving.

The first is associated with a church that I was attending, where I knew, via dreams and visions, had issues with its leadership. I not only had these dreams and visions, but I also overheard various comments, which was basically, gossip about the husband and wife who were pastors of the church.

One day, I felt prompt to make a vow to give $10,000 to the church. It was the first time that I felt lead to write out a vow, which was immediately after hearing the needs of the church. I must honestly say, it was either God or deception because my thoughts were, why would God tell me to give to a church where I knew that the pastor was doing ungodly things related to the ministry and especially towards his wife. But nonetheless, I made the vow.

About two weeks later, I received a check in the mail for $10,340. I can't remember where the money came from, but I asked the Lord, "May I cash the check so I could keep the $340 portion of the check?" I felt as if He crossed his arms and said, "Really!" The following Sunday, the pastor had me come up to the front of the church in order for him to announce that I had kept my vow. As I extended my arm to hand him the check, he looked me in my eyes and asked, "Are you sure?" As he took the check, I fell to my knees and cried. Not because I just gave away over $10,000, but I had no idea if I was being deceived or was it God. But what I do remember saying "God I know you will honor my desire to serve and please you and you alone."

Forty-two hours later, I received another check for $10,430. Remember, I gave $10,340 but then received another check that had the same numbers. I remember crying and praising God with the check in my hand. He said to me, "Do not look at who you are giving to, just listen to me and let me judge, not you." This was one lesson that I will never forget.

When God leads us to give, He is not only preparing us to receive, but He wants us to know that we are not giving to 'man', but we are giving to Him. Whether the person honors the funds or not, at the end of the day they will be held accountable to God. We simply need to be accountable to God as it relates to our giving.

Please know that I am 'not' advocating giving to false prophets, unethical pastors, or snake oil charmers.[24] You need to be open and willing to hear God tell you to give. Some people ask whether I believe in tithing. I have a long story about that as well. However, the short of it is, one day, while I was in California, God woke me up and said, "**You owe me money!**" I then felt like I was supposed to calculate the amount of money I had made, after being saved, and give that total number to the church I was attending as well as different people that I knew. Let's just say, it was a substantial amount and I felt complete joy in doing so.

There are people who believe that the tithe or 10 percent of one's wages is an Old Testament principle. My question is, would you rather give 10 percent or, 'all', which *is* a New Testament principle? Giving and living like Jesus requires that you realize He did not give 10%, 20% or even 99%, but all of who He was and still is.

When you read the New Testament, it never gives a certain percentage as an obligatory standard for our giving. When it refers to 10%, it is always referring to an Old Testament scripture. However, the New Testament declares:

> *Let each one do just as he has purposed in his heart; not grudgingly or under compulsion; for God loves a cheerful giver. (2 Corinthians 9:7).*

You have to remember that the Old Testament tithe was required by law. The Jews were under compulsion to give it, while the New Testament teaching on giving focuses on it being a joyous and voluntary act:

---

[24]Snake oil is an expression that originally referred to fraudulent health products or unproven medicine but has come to refer to any product with questionable or unverifiable quality or benefit. By extension, a snake oil salesman is someone who knowingly sells fraudulent goods or who is themselves a fraud, quack, charlatan, or the like

For I testify that according to their ability, and beyond their ability they gave of their own accord. (2 Corinthians 8:3).

This voluntary giving is exactly what Abraham and Jacob were doing before the institution of the Law, and is what all Christians are to do today. *Believers today are free to give the amount they choose to give, while making sure that their giving is pleasing to the Lord, which might not be pleasing to their budget.*

I cannot count the amount of times that I clearly heard the Lord say "Empty your wallet!" Or wake me up at night in order to wire thousands overseas to a ministry of a person that I barely knew, or even give money to someone I encountered at a gas station.

I also cannot count the number of times someone came up to me and gave me money. But what I can tell you is the number of times that God had me forward the money, someone gave me, to someone else, burn a seven thousand dollar check, or simply send back hundreds of dollars, I felt I wasn't supposed to receive. All I do know is when God said give, He is and will always be the one, 'using' me to get His resources to who He specifies.

The second testimony has to do with receiving over $20,000 checks in the mail, when it were not expected, or even receiving a $70,000 check in the mail after giving everything I had in my bank account, which was a little over $300. I remember hearing a minister say, *"If the money you have does not meet your need, then it is a seed!"* Meaning, if the money you have does not pay your bills, buy your food, or sustain you for the month, then find a place, a church, or someone to sow it into, knowing that what you have sown, you shall reap. And, please know that this is not a 'give and take' scheme, but a principle of God…. He loves a cheerful giver, so you need to make sure that your attitude is cheerful indeed.

Giving is not only about giving hundreds and thousands of dollars, it is simply about obeying God, even if it's a quarter ($0.25).

The third testimony is associated with the time I had listened to a minister, who happened to also be an accountant. He told a story about

God telling him to give another minister dirt. Yes, you read that right, 'dirt'. He shared that he was willing to give money, or even a really nice gift, but God kept confirming that it should be dirt. Of course he obeyed God and the gift of 'dirt' was a blessing to the recipient.

Well, God did not tell me to give dirt, but 25¢ to a man who is head of an international mission's organization. It was after listening to him share that he wanted to have a crusade in America, similar to those in other countries. It was the last day I was in the US, prior to returning to South Korea, which meant I did not have a lot of finances, in dollars, to give. So, instead of giving dollars, I put all of the Korean won in the offering envelope and left. You do realize I was in complete 'disobedience' to God's directive.

After leaving the conference, and arriving to the international airport, I went to the ladies room. While in the ladies room, I began to feel the fear of the Lord. I didn't hear God, but I knew it had to do with the 25¢. It was as if God was saying, "Didn't I tell you to give him 25¢?" Honestly, I knew it was the Holy Spirit. The best way to describe this is, for those of you who have siblings and your parents told all of you not to do something, and you do it anyway. Your siblings give you that 'look' knowing that you are going to be in trouble once your parents are made aware of what you have done.

Well, as I was walking out of the bathroom, back into the main area of the airport, in the threshold of the bathroom and the hall, I looked down and guess what was on the floor, a quarter, a 25¢ coin.

I left out that bathroom so fast and prayed, "God please don't let me die in a state of disobedience!" When I confessed what I did to my friend, we were both speechless.

Once I arrived back to South Korea, I began to unpack and catch up on work. I told myself that I would go out the following day to the post office and mail the quarter because I needed to do laundry as well.

After putting my clothes in the washing machine, I sat at my desk in order to get some work done. After some time, I heard the washing machine beeping. The beeping lasted longer than the normal length of time indicating that the load had finished.

When the beeping went past a minute, I got up to check the washing machine. *THE WASHING MACHINE STOPPED WORKING, AND* **25** *WAS BLINKING ON THE FRONT OF THE MACHINE!!!!* Within 15 minutes I wrote a letter apologizing for being disobedient and ran out to mail the quarter. I asked God what was that all about, but I did not receive an answer.

A few months later, my accountant informed me, that I had a problem with the IRS. The problem was, 'they owed me money'. In addition, a few days prior to the accountant's information, I received an email stating that I was owed money from a project I had worked on earlier in the year. Can you guess how much everything totaled? A little over $25,000!

Did the quarter have anything to do with the $25,000? Did the $10,430, have anything to do with the $10,340? Did the $300 have anything to do with the $70,000? I honestly believe that it is all connected. Do I believe that you need to be a Christian to be wealthy? After working with millionaires who want nothing to do with God, but have more money than entire congregations, it is obvious that you don't have to believe in God in order to be wealthy. But, I have never met a millionaire who goes to sleep in a blissful state of peace, without knowing Jesus Christ.

Faith and Deeds

14 What good is it, my brothers and sisters, if someone claims to have faith but has no deeds? Can such faith save them? 15 Suppose a brother or a sister is without clothes and daily food. 16 If one of you says to them, "Go in peace; keep warm and well fed," but does nothing about their physical needs, what good is it? 17 In the same way, faith by itself, if it is not accompanied by action, is dead.

18 But someone will say, "You have faith; I have deeds." Show me your faith without deeds, and I will show you my faith by my deeds. 19 You believe that there is one God. Good! Even the demons believe that—and shudder. 20 You foolish person, do you want evidence that faith without deeds is useless? 21 Was not our father Abraham considered righteous for what he did when he offered his son Isaac on the altar? 22 You see that his faith and his actions were working together, and his faith was made complete by what he did. 23 And the scripture was fulfilled that says, "Abraham believed God, and it was credited to him as righteousness," and he was called God's friend. 24 You see that a person is considered righteous by what they do and not by faith alone. 25 In the same way, was not even Rahab the prostitute considered righteous for what she did when she gave lodging to the spies and sent them off in a different direction? 26 As the body without the spirit is dead, so faith without deeds is dead. (James 2:14-26)

Running

Jesus Has Risen

When the Sabbath was over, Mary Magdalene, Mary the mother of James, and Salome bought spices so that they might go to anoint Jesus' body. 2 Very early on the first day of the week, just after sunrise, they were on their way to the tomb 3 and they asked each other, "Who will roll the stone away from the entrance of the tomb?"

4 But when they looked up, they saw that the stone, which was very large, had been rolled away. 5 As they entered the tomb, they saw a young man dressed in a white robe sitting on the right side, and they were alarmed. 6 "Don't be alarmed," he said. "You are looking for Jesus the Nazarene, who was crucified. He has risen! He is not here. See the place where they laid him. 7 But go, tell his disciples and Peter, 'He is going ahead of you into Galilee. There you will see him, just as he told you.'" 8 Trembling and bewildered, the women went out and fled from the tomb. They said nothing to anyone, because they were afraid.

[The earliest manuscripts and some other ancient witnesses do not have verses 9– 20.]

9 When Jesus rose early on the first day of the week, he appeared first to Mary Magdalene, out of whom he had driven seven demons. 10 She went and told those who had been with him and who were mourning and weeping. 11 When they heard that Jesus was alive and that she had seen him, they did not believe it. 12 Afterward Jesus appeared in a different form to two of them while they were walking in the country. 13 These returned and reported it to the rest; but they did not believe them either.

14 Later Jesus appeared to the Eleven as they were eating; he rebuked them for their lack of faith and their stubborn refusal to believe those who had seen him after he had risen. 15 He said to them, "Go into all the world and preach the gospel to all creation. 16 Whoever believes and is baptized will be saved, but whoever does not believe will be condemned. 17 And these signs will accompany those who believe: In my name they will drive out demons; they will speak in new tongues; 18 they will pick up snakes with their hands; and when they drink deadly poison, it will not hurt them at all; they will place their hands on sick people, and they will get well."

19 After the Lord Jesus had spoken to them, he was taken up into heaven and he sat at the right hand of God. 20 Then the disciples went out and preached everywhere, and the Lord worked with them and confirmed his word by the signs that accompanied it. (Mark 16: 1-20)

Returning to South Korea

No longer having a job wasn't something that I thought I would be facing, even though I had been praying about not working as well as spending more time reading the Word and enjoying doing all that God was calling me to do. But, the realization that I would not have a steady income put me in a mindset that was full of anticipation and excitement. This was because I had enough savings, where all of my bills would be taken care of, for three years. My mortgage, car loan, student loans, and credit card bills, would all be paid on time, with the savings I had accumulated over the years. I could even pay off all of my credit card debt and still have money remaining to live comfortably. I could continue to travel, go where God was telling me to go, and give what He was telling me to give. However, God had other plans for 'His' savings.

God began to have me write very large checks to missionaries, ministries and even to complete strangers. I was sent to South Africa, Nigeria, Italy, and a host of other places, while continuously giving away thousands of dollars.

The first few months were exciting as I was in South Africa one week, then Nigeria the following week. I realized that it was during this time that God was showing me that no matter how wealthy, or poor, *everyone* needs Jesus.

While in South Africa, I was staying in Sandton Square also known as Mandela's Square. It is one of South Africa's leading and most prestigious shopping centers in Sandton which is an affluent area situated within the metro area of Johannesburg, Gauteng, South Africa. It is also known as 'Africa's Richest Square Mile".

I realized prior to being sent to Nigeria, South Africa and London, all within a months' time, that He had been preparing me, by telling me where to go within blocks of my home, then to different cities, and different states, and now different countries. I did not realize during those times, that He was preparing me for more than just going to a different country for a temporary missionary assignment.

It was immediately after returning from my 2nd trip to Israel that God told me to move to South Korea. In all honesty, given the fact that I had visited South Korea while traveling throughout Asia, my first response was, "God, Koreans don't like Black people!" I not only thought this, I said it out loud.

I had not read any stories about racism in South Korea, nor had I heard about South Koreans being racist, all I knew was during my three months of traveling throughout Asia, South Korea was the only country I 'vowed' never to return.

Being an African-American who had a very unconventional lifestyle, meaning, even though I grew up in a drug-invested area of the Bronx in New York City, I was in specialized academic programs for the intellectually gifted, I started taking college courses at the age of 14, started my first business at 16, and started working on Wall Street by the time I was18 years old. I had mastered dealing with American style racism and did not want to deal with it in Asia. Does this debate in my heart sound familiar to the beginning of this book.

When God told me to move to South Korea, four years had passed since being saved and God directing me to stay on Wall Street. During those four years, He had taken me to Africa, Europe, and various cities in America, in order to be a blessing, and receive blessings from others. Those blessings came in the form of teaching, hands-on training, receiving and giving money, and the best of all, developing friendships.

And yet, there I was, lying in bed responding to Him as if I had just met Him.

The real problem that I had was the fact that it was near the end of 2008, and by this time, I had given away all of the funds in my retirement accounts, all of my savings, and cleared out all of my investment accounts. However, I had just signed contracts with three different organizations that were going to pay me substantially, once their projects took off. He told me to cancel all of the contracts and simply, trust Him!

There are a lot of details involved in transitioning from America to South Korea, but from the day He told me to move to the day I boarded the plane, it was exactly three months. The various details are laid out in, *Send Me I Will Go*, but I will share one specific story about how I bought…excuse me… how 'He' bought my plane ticket.

It was between 2am-3am in the morning, when He woke me up and told me to call a specific airline. While waiting for someone to answer, after going pass the automated portion of the system, the first person I spoke to was clearly angry. When she answered the phone, it sounded like she was growling, "Hello Blank Airlines, how may I help you!" I responded with a, "No Thank You", and hung up. I took a minute, prayed and then called back. The woman who answered had the sweetest voice.

"Hello, thank you for calling Blank Airlines, this is Ceci, how may I help you?" After telling her what I needed, she proceeded to search for a ticket. As she searched, she asked me why I was going to South Korea. By that time, I had gotten tired of people telling me that I was crazy to be going to Asia. Some people even said, "You are Black, why won't God send you to Africa for missions?" My response to her was simply, "To travel."

As she was giving me the prices of the very expensive ticket, I could hear her mobile ring in the background. She quickly apologized and put me on hold, however, I could hear her talking and referring to the person as 'sweetheart'. She was talking to her child.

After she came back on the phone, I asked her if everything was okay, and she explained that she had a sick child at home. I got excited and then confessed that it was God who was sending me to South Korea for missions. I explained how it was supposed to be my missions' base and I would most likely be serving in different parts of Asia. After sharing this with her, I told her that I believed that God had me call her, not for the ticket but to pray for her, and her daughter. As she cried over the phone, she proceeded to tell me that earlier during the day, she 'said', "God if you are real, can you please help my daughter", and there I was calling.

After praying and talking a little more, I was about to hang up thinking that was the reason God had me call that specific airline, at that specific time. But before I could hang up, she reminded me that I had called for a ticket.

I shared with her that I did not have a lot of money, but I knew God was having me call the airline for her. With hesitation, she said, "Hold on a minute!" I said, okay, and proceeded to get excited because I knew God was going to do something amazing.

She comes back on the phone and told me, that she was able to get the ticket that was originally $2,100, down to about $1,700 with a number of lengthy layovers.

I informed Ceci that I had about $300 to my name because God had me give most of my money away. She responded with, "Hold on again." At that point, I was doing backflips and somersaults, I was not only excited, but the angels in my room were more excited. Yes, angels!

When Ceci came back onto the line, she asked, "How about $60.10?" I could not contain my excitement. This ticket was bought for a trip that would take place, within three weeks. I thanked her profusely, and she thanked me as well.

As I recall that day, I am now realizing that God supernaturally encountered me on an airplane, coming back to America. And in order for me to leave America, He was supernaturally taking me to another country that would be my home.

Prior to that phone call, I cannot count the amount of people who said I should not go, and gave me hundreds of reasons. Most reminded me of the fact that I didn't speak the language, didn't have a place to live or work, and questioned how was I going to make money.

Other reasons included; you are not married, you should not travel alone, you are a single woman, and you are a single Black woman, what will you do if war breaks out, what will you do if North Korea bombs South Korea, are you sure this is God because this doesn't sound right? God wouldn't have you do this, leave your big house, cancel your clients' contracts, leave A.M.E.R.I.C.A where opportunities abound! All of the, 'what ifs' were based in fear. To be honest, until I wrote the above, I did not realize that the same things people said when I told them I was moving to California, were some of the same things they said upon my announcement that I was moving to South Korea. Different specifics, but the exact same thing...*you should be afraid to obey God and go to a place you have never gone before.*

All I knew was that I was not going to be someone who was going to succumb to the fears of 'man'. Yes, I knew that my family, friends, and church members cared for me, but no Christian should proceed according to man's knowledge of right and wrong. I had learned, and was yet, still learning to do everything out of sheer obedience to God, because I loved Him and trusted Him more than I trusted anyone else...even myself.

It was during this transition from America to South Korea that I learned that the principle of discerning good and evil is the principle of living by what God says is right and wrong.

Before Adam and Eve took the fruit, their understanding of right and wrong were in God. If they did not live before God, they knew nothing; both their right and wrong were just God Himself. But after they ate from the tree of the *Knowledge of Good and Evil,* they found a source of discerning between right and wrong apart from God. As a consequence, after man's fall, there was no need to seek after God. They could get along by themselves, and even isolate themselves from God and judge between right and wrong. This ultimately was *The Fall.* But it is the redemptive work of Jesus Christ that restores our relationship and communication back to God, who tells us what is right and what is wrong; which way we should go and how long we should stay.

While going through this, I realized that I didn't need a person's opinion or their deductive reasoning given the limited facts they had, I needed to hear God different, and/or hear God from those who covered me in prayer. If I had not learned that the greatest demand by God is being fully submitted to His will, I would not be sitting here, seven years later, living in South Korea, and editing this book while traveling between France and Israel.

Before you pack your bags to run off to another country, or another city, I must share that I have met very few people who simply hear God, and go. Meaning, they are not lone rangers that 'only' listen for God's voice. Obeying God looks like a person who 'hears' God for themselves, and are surrounded by people who love and obey God as well. These are the people who provide 'Godly' counsel prior to our execution of God's directives.

There are no opinions, no 'what do you think,' no 'how do you feel about the situation questions'. It's should always be about, "what did you hear God say?" I have also learned that God does not share His plans for 'your' life with everyone. He graces those you are to share with. So, He will 'only' speak to those that have His heart for your situation.

Whatever plan God has for your life, you must ensure that you determine in your mind and heart that "His will, will be done."

When you come to a point in your life where others are your primary concern (I am not talking about neglecting yourself, and living as a self-sacrificing victim), but one whose focus is on God and God's will, it is then, and only then, that He uses you to manifest who He is for others, while at the same time meeting all of your needs as well.

People often ask me "How do you make sure if you are supposed to go to a certain country, take on a specific ministry assignment, or even go to a Christian training program/conference?" I share the fact that I have met so many people where they talk about doing something for 'God's kingdom' and yet they never mentioned how it would benefit someone outside of themselves. They have shared how they obtained their M.Div., spent a year or two doing various ministry training activities, and have attended quite a few conferences... over a ten year period… and yet, have shared the gospel with no more than five people, if that many.

I have met church goers who have all of the retreats, parties, picnics, movie nights, and even prayer meetings that are focused on their prayer needs, and yet do absolutely nothing for anyone else. Does the once a month or twice a year orphanage visit count? What about feeding the homeless during the various holiday sessions? Does any of these acts that show 'your kindness' mean anything? Well, only God can tell you that. But what He does say is…

James 1:27 The Message (MSG) 26-27 Anyone who sets himself up as "religious" by talking a good game is self-deceived. This kind of religion is hot air and only hot air. Real religion, the kind that passes muster before God the Father, is this: Reach out to the homeless and loveless in their plight, and guard against corruption from the godless world.

If you are going to walk in obedience to God by going to different events and training courses, then you want to make sure that your heart is positioned to receive, in order to be equipped to do the 'work' of the ministry. This doesn't refer to simply holding a position in a church or a religious institution. I am referring to being prepared and equipped to share the gospel with the person in the cubicle next to you. It is great to be equipped and excited to lay hands on the sick, raise the dead, and *do* all that Jesus has empowered us to do, even while you are on the phone booking airline tickets, or when a telemarketer calls you. But you must be prepared to market the One that they all need. So the next time a telemarketer calls you, before you hang up, share Christ.

A Heart For India

In certain Christian circles, especially among those who have gone to other nations, we all know that if there is a country, or even a culture we 'feel some-which-way' about, God will take us and sit us right in the middle of it. As previously discussed, South Korea was one of two nations that I vowed never to return. However, after being saved for some years, there were two other countries, I unknowingly developed a fear of visiting, one of them being India.

I had been to places in Asia and Africa where the effects of witchcraft and the demonic were not only tangible, and the molecular make-up of the atmosphere was like pudding, but it was a life long acceptable state of existence for people in those regions. Unfortunately, the presence of evil was so very evident, not only in the atmosphere, but in the way people treated each other. But, even in those nations, the presence of Christ would dispel the evil, even from the darkest of places, and soften the hardest of hearts. Yet, when I thought of India, all I could think of were the testimonies from, 'well seasoned' and powerful Christians, about their bouts with the demonic. I have met people who have shared some of the 'craziest' stories, but then and again, they could say the same thing about my stories from my time in South Korea.

I remember going to a gathering in Seoul and meeting a young Korean woman who was a missionary in the other nation I did not want to travel to. As she and I talked, she stated emphatically that the spiritual atmosphere in South Korea was more intense than the country we were discussing. That was the day that I knew I believed a lie and allowed the fear of a nation and its very real spiritual activity, to prevent God's love from flowing in my heart and mind, for the people of that nation.

This is a tactic of the enemy that some come into agreement with, which keeps us bound by lies about nations and people groups. After meeting that young woman, it was a few months later that God took me to the nation where the notion of 330 million gods is accepted.[25]

Remember when I discovered Benny Hinn's ministry while in California?[26] You will recall that I had noted that I thought he was an 'Indian' man. It wasn't just because of the way he looked and how he sounded, but he was ministering to thousands of Indians.

You might be asking, "How does this story about India, connect with South Korea?" Well, till this day, I do not know how Benny Hinn Ministries (BHM) found my address in South Korea. I honestly do not remember sowing into his ministry using my debit card from my bank in South Korea because I keep track of my gift giving with my American accounts. But, I received a package from BHM while my friend Chazaline was visiting.

I picked up my mail and went to my office in order to prepare for lectures. Weeks prior to this, I had a conversation with a friend, Janet,

---

[25]I am not going to go into a lot of details here, but to help those who keep repeating that Indians believe in 330 million gods, in Hinduism, there are actually only, 33 gods. This transition from 33 to 330 million came after, what is called the Upanishadic Age. Upanishads taught that ultimate reality is a single supreme soul, called Brahman. The count went to millions in an attempt to express the infinitude of the universe, to capture the all-pervading reality. This is how 330 million gods made sense. They believe that god is not someone sitting in the clouds giving out justice. He is in everything in this creation. He is more than this creation. Without the existence of that principle called god, him, you, and I cannot exist. So when they say there are 330 million gods, it is because you and I are also expressions of god. We are some of the 330 million plus ways god is expressing / manifesting himself.
[26]Chapter: Benny Hinn: The Indian Man

who I had met while attending church in Seoul. Her parents, Dan and Marlene were in India building and giving away houses to the poor and widows in an area outside of Chennai. Janet had shared some of her parent's journey about how they went from South Africa to Hawaii, and eventually, God placed them both in India. I remember thinking, WOW, better them than me!

A few weeks after Janet shared the story about her parents, while sitting at my desk at home, I had a vision of Marlene, Janet's mom, being up in clouds. There were a couple of other things, but the point was, I never met her parents, nor had I seen a picture of them. Yet, I knew it was Marlene. I called Janet to tell her about the vision.

Janet informed me that her mom was heading up into the mountains with another friend, and there was some trepidation, however, the vision was a reassurance that Marlene would be protected. It was at this point in time that I felt God was telling me to 'Go to India'. But, I hid this in my heart with a 'God you will have to tell me exactly when to go and where to go'...not realizing that a life changing event was about to take place.

How does this story relate to the BHM's package? Just a couple of weeks after this vision, my friend Chazaline came to visit, and the day after her arrival was when I received the package.

After I finished my lectures, Chazaline met me in my office and we began to catch up with each other. I had shared with her what had happened with Janet's mom and we began to feel the presence of the Lord. After we finished talking, I started to open up my mail, including the BHM envelope. It was a DVD of Benny Hinn, in *INDIA* and it was the crusade I had seen on television while I was in my kitchen in California. We all know what happened next. Let's just say, those of you who have had those God encounters where you start to cry, laugh, wail, and everything else, began to take place in my office. That was when I knew that I needed to go to India and serve with Dan and Marlene.

After sharing with Janet all that had transpired, she connected me to her parents. A couple of weeks later, I bought my ticket, and made all of the arrangements to spend one month in Mamallapuram, Tamil Nadu, India, which is about 60 km south the city of Chennai.

There were so many encounters while in India. The stories are detailed in *Spiritual Warfare, A Fight for Love.*© I must be honest and say that I was waiting to see the demonic manifest itself, similar to what I had seen in other nations. But, as I traveled the streets, ate with locals, met people, and served with Dan and Marlene, I saw nothing. I did not see any demonic oppression similar to what I had become accustomed to in South Korea. I did not see dragons following people around, or what looked like dead people walking alongside people. I did not see witches astral projecting in and out of people's houses or their cars. Nor did I see the rage and anger in the eyes of the poorest of people, or those who were considered wealthy. I also did not encounter any Indian related spiritual attacks. I did not feel threatened, even though the rides in the Tut-tuts were ones to remember.[27] All I saw were hundreds of people who were as innocent as children, who were going through their daily lives.

The sun will not smite you by day, Nor the moon by night. The LORD will protect you from all evil; He will keep your soul. The LORD will guard your going out and your coming in From this time forth and forever. (Psalms 121:6-8)

The LORD protects and preserves them-- they are counted among the blessed in the land- he does not give them over to the desire of their foes. (Psalm 41:2).

I must share that even though I did not encounter any Indian related spiritual attacks, I did have one hair-raising encounter that I will share at another time.

Were the stories that I heard about India real? Of course they were. Is the spiritual atmosphere in India any less evil than in Africa, the Americas, or South Korea? Of course not! One must remember, that

---

[27] An auto rickshaw, also known as a three-wheeler. It's a common form of urban transport, both as a vehicle for hire and for private use, in many countries around the world, especially those with tropical or subtropical climates.

where ever there are households, a city, a state, or country that does not want God, but practices worshiping animals, things, or people, by actively engaging in diverse rituals associated with calling on the dead, you will have evil prevailing... until God invades, either supernaturally, or through 'You'.

On the other hand, I cannot put into words the love that overwhelmed my heart for everyone I met. I can still remember the men and women who excitedly asked about touching my hair, due to the fact that they had never seen my hair type, "up close and personal", as they had stated.

When God has planned for you to go to a nation, or even down the block to love on someone by sharing the gospel of His kingdom, "Go!" If He tugs at your heart to go to a nation, or even a people group that you know have an issue with you being a woman, a man, rich, poor, or a certain race, I guarantee you, He will be with you and He will cover you. By God putting you in what would be considered dangerous environments, it is then and only then, that there is a demand on all of your training, the gifts God has given you, and most importantly, the love He has empowered you with.

Being in India broke down a lot of the lies that I had hidden in my heart. As previously noted, I was simply afraid of the known spiritual climate in the region. Which does not make 'logical' sense being that I had lived in and traveled to over 30 nations prior to going to India. I can tell you some stories where, because of the presence of evil, God in all His majesty prevailed in ways that my heart is even now rejoicing over.

Most people who proclaim to be Christians, will not admit that they do not want to go to a certain nation, or people group due to having an obstinate, irrational, unfair intolerance of ideas, opinions, and even hate towards those who are different from them. What they don't realize is that they are disobeying the most important commandant that Jesus gave, outside of love God with all your heart, mind and soul... and that is to love your neighbor.

Loving your neighbor as Christ loves you does not mean willingly and habitually engaging in, and accepting behavior that is antithetical to the Biblical principles Christ set for God's creation to live by. Nor does it mean ignoring those who are practicing such behavior by making statements similar to what I have heard Christians say, "It's their life, if they want to do it, it is their right." "Everyone should be free to do what they want, when they want, how they want, and with who they want." Statements like these are nowhere to be found in the Bible, they are actually associated with secular humanism which postulates that human beings are capable of being ethical and moral without religion or a god. Secular humanism does not assume that humans are either inherently evil or innately good, nor does it present humans as being superior to nature. Rather, the humanist life stance emphasizes the unique responsibility facing humanity and the ethical consequences of human decisions. Fundamental to the concept of secular humanism is the strongly held viewpoint that ideology—be it religious or political—must be thoroughly examined by each individual and not simply accepted or rejected on faith.[28]

A Christian is someone who does not accept the beliefs of those who are living in sin and darkness. A Christian is one who does accept and love people who choose to live in a state of sin and darkness. Acceptance does not mean, you cheer one on as they engage in self-destructive behavior that either keeps them from living an abundant life here on earth, while ensuring that they will live one of torture for eternity once they die. Every Christian is to do exactly what Jesus Christ did, engage and speak truth towards everyone who has yet to receive Him.

The Most Important Commandment

28 One of the religion scholars came up. Hearing the lively exchanges of question and answer and seeing how sharp Jesus was in his answers, he put in his question: "Which is most important of all the commandments?"

---

[28] Secular humanism. (2015, December 7).What Is Secular Humanism? http://www.christiananswers.net/q-sum/sum-r002.html

29-31 Jesus said, "The first in importance is, 'Listen, Israel: The Lord your God is one; so love the Lord God with all your passion and prayer and intelligence and energy.' And here is the second: 'Love others as well as you love yourself.' There is no other commandment that ranks with these."

32-33 The religion scholar said, "A wonderful answer, Teacher! So lucid and accurate—that God is one and there is no other. And loving him with all passion and intelligence and energy, and loving others as well as you love yourself. Why, that's better than all offerings and sacrifices put together!" 34 When Jesus realized how insightful he was, he said, "You're almost there, right on the border of God's kingdom." (Mark 12: 28-34 Message version).

Heading Towards God... But Away From God

Over the years, I have learned that God doesn't want us to simply be robots who obey Him. He desires for us to find joy in obeying His leading as we walk on the path that He has laid out for us. May that path be filled with people who are serving others around the world, or those filled with hate for themselves and others, it is all about being in His perfect will.

This walk with God is always eventful. There will always be some really good surprises and there are some that will make you want to crawl into bed and pull the covers over your head. I have had my share of days of pulling the covers over my head, as if God couldn't see me. The story I am about to share was one such occasion.

I can count a number of times where I felt like God had to 'pick me up' or lovingly 'shout' at me to ensure that there were no mental gymnastics as it related to what He wanted me to do. I had already traveled to a number of nations, preached in places that clearly did not want the Lord, and walked with people who pretended to want Him but in reality simply wanted His 'fish and loaves', as the next events started to take place, I knew I was in for another action-packed ride.

I had spent five years working at a 'Christian' university in South Korea. I had settled into the notion that I would be there for a number of years because I was believing for revival to break out, not only on the campus, but also in the city in which the university was located.

There were a number of prophetic words I had received, as well as visions as it related to a move of God on the hearts of the young and old. I had even discovered a church that was filled with people who loved God and allowed the Holy Spirit to have His way in their church services.

They prayed regularly for the president of Korea to love God, for the students to have a heart after God and not after grades and positions. They prayed for marriages, families, and simply for everyone in the nations of North and South Korea to not only love God, but to receive the Father's heart for their lives. They also believed in walking people through healing and deliverance. Not medicating mental problems, or counseling people, but allowing God to heal and deliver people of everything that had them bound.

I discovered the church by being invited to hear a guest speaker. It was also during the same month I was leaving for Texas to be ordained. I never thought, or had a desire to be ordained. I did not think that there was anything wrong with being ordained, or the ordination process. However, I strongly felt that there were churches, as well as various religious organizations that developed a number of non-God policies and procedures that presented too many hoops for people to simply go and obey God. In addition to that, I had never encountered a demon possessed person, or a person who needed God to heal them, or provide them with food and safe drinking water, ask me to show them my ordination papers. But, nonetheless, I obeyed and was ordained by a ministry that has spent decades, training and equipping believers to take the healing power of God beyond church walls and into every part of the earth.

Before moving on, 'Yes', I belonged to a church in South Korea, as well as maintain a relationship with a church I still consider my home church in America. However, I do realize that when God moves us into another realm of engaging people and places, He provides us with not only the covering we need, but the people who have encountered similar situations who can pray accordingly for us as well.

The day after returning to South Korea from Texas, I was informed that the department that I had worked with was going to be phased out and merged with another school that is under the umbrella of the university. It's an academic structure in South Korea where a Korean university opens another college where the entire curriculum is taught in English, and the school caters to students from around the world.

During a meeting with my department, with the powers that be at the university, and faculty from the college, we were all told we should not worry about our jobs and that we will all be working together in order to develop a global program that attracts students from around the world. The meeting was held on a Monday. Four days later, I received a call from the dean of my department stating that he wanted to come to my office.

During the five years of being at the university, the dean had never visited my office. Not knowing what was going on, actually, not having a clue, or even feeling a 'Holy Spirit- heads up', I met him in my office.

Upon seeing him, his head was down and he looked sullen. I asked if he was okay and he proceeded to tell me that the university would not be renewing my contract because the class I was responsible for teaching was no longer being offered with the new curriculum. He then proceeded to tell me that I had to write a letter of resignation. I responded that I was not going to write a letter of resignation because I would be lying.

Being unable to look at me, he continued to apologize and wasn't sure what else to say other than push the issue of writing a letter of resignation. The dean proceeded to tell me that he would try to get me moved to another department at the university, or over to the college in order for me to stay with the university. I found out a few weeks later that, one of the many unethical things that universities in South Korea do to foreign professors, who have been at the school for five years or more is, they attempt to get them to write a letter of resignation because it is "against the law to not renew a contract of a professor who had worked five years, or more for the university". I must say I was shocked because, in 2010 God placed me at this specific university, after telling me to leave the university I was previously with. Again, because of a number of unethical actions the university was taking.

In order to make the timeline of events clear, Monday was the faculty meeting, Friday was the encounter with the dean. On Sunday, my pastor preached a message called, "Coming out of Egypt." He asked, "Do you automatically want to go to Egypt when it comes to getting a job....?" "Do you automatically want to go back to Egypt in your emotions when it comes to your husband, wife, or children, doing everything like the Egyptians and those in the world in order to handle the different problems that come up in life?" *As I wrote earlier, I found a Holy Spirit led church, and a pastor who not only preached amazing sermons, but he, 'consistently' listened and shared the logos and rhema word of the Lord.*

He ended the message by asking, "Are we relying on Egypt for all the things that God says He will provide?"

Two weeks later, on a Monday, as I was heading to the dean's office to find out if he had spoken to the other colleges, I must admit that I was doing all the calculations in my head as it related to the cost of rent/monthly bills and the nemesis in my life, my six figure student loan bill. However, once I reached the floor of his office, I heard my pastor's voice as if he was in the hallway with me, "Are you going to Egypt for help?" And, Isaiah 30:1-5 started to repeat in my mind....

Futile Confidence in Egypt

1 "Woe to the rebellious children," says the Lord, "Who take counsel, but not of me, and who devise plans, but not of My Spirit, That they may add sin to sin;

2 Who walk to go down to Egypt, and have not asked my advice, To strengthen themselves in the strength of Pharaoh, And to trust in the shadow of Egypt!

3 Therefore the strength of Pharaoh shall be your shame, and trust in the shadow of Egypt shall be your humiliation. 4 For his princes were at Zoan, and his ambassadors came to Hanes. 5 They were all ashamed of a people who could not benefit them, or be help or benefit, but a shame and also a reproach." Isaiah 30:1-5 (NKJV)

Here is how the Message version presents it:

All Show, No Substance

30 1-5 "Doom, rebel children!" God's Decree! "You make plans, but not mine. You make deals, but not in my Spirit. You pile sin on sin, one sin on top of another, going off to Egypt without so much as asking me, running off to Pharaoh for protection, expecting to hide out in Egypt. Well, some protection Pharaoh will be! Some hideout, Egypt! They look big and important, true, with officials strategically established in Zoan in the north and Hanes in the south, but there's nothing to them. Anyone stupid enough to trust them will end up looking stupid. All show, no substance, an embarrassing farce."

I knew it was God reminding me of the sermon and the scriptures. And, as soon as I reached his door, I did about-face[29] and went home.

As I walked down my prayer path, which is a path that passes missionary homes that were built in the 1950s by missionaries who were establishing the university, I asked God for forgiveness and to help my heart and mind be completely focused on Him and not the circumstances. Once I arrived home, I had not one, but two checks in the mail. Then, the following Wednesday, after finding out that the college was not going to hire new professors, I arrived home and there was another check!

All three checks totaled close to 70% of my annual income from the university.

---

[29]. The act of pivoting to face in the opposite direction from the original, especially in a military formation. A military command to turn clockwise 180°. A total change of attitude or viewpoint. about-face. (n.d.) *American Heritage® Dictionary of the English Language, Fifth Edition.* (2011).

Then last but not least, a few days later, I received a phone call from the dean at the college wanting me to send my resume directly to him! He said that they were approved to hire a professor with a Ph.D. in International Business. If they couldn't find someone, then I will be hired. I must admit that I was happy and disgusted at the same time.

My thoughts were, I have been at the university for five years, never missed a day, never showed up late to a class, met with hundreds of students for various reasons outside the scope of my class, had the highest evaluations, and yet, "*...if we don't find someone else, then we will give you the position.*" Yup, that is Egypt for you.

As I now type this, I must add that my friend Chazaline was visiting again. As I shared about all of my options, she looked at me and said, "It is time for you to move on." I knew that it was indeed time for me to move on. There were a host of other hoops that appeared during the two-month saga, from being offered the position with the college, to not getting a contract, to running around to get certain documents. I have a saying "*Don't complain about getting stabbed in the back if you keep sharpening the knife and giving it to the person, turning around, and allowing them to stab you.*"

We always have a choice to respond in faith or respond to all the foolishness transpiring. This is something we all know. We all know that when things start to shift, we must determine if it's God steering things, or is it the devil coming into kill, steal, destroy, interrupt, or delay God's plans. The problem is, when we are not at peace, especially in our mind, we can't determine if it's God or the enemy.

Why do we need to know who is responsible for what is happening? This determines how we are to pray. If we have to take our spiritual warfare stance and go into battle, then fight is what we must do. But if it's God rearranging things, we cannot war against the One who has plans for us. Even if we can see the enemy using those who are closest to us, to lie, cheat, or even manipulate the process, God is still the one who knows where He wants us to be. Our responsibility is to keep our eyes, mind, heart, actions, and most importantly, '*mouth*' focused on God.

As I began to pray, as well as look for another position, I began to get offers from other universities within a week of sending out my resume. I wasn't concerned with getting a 'job', I was focused on hearing God direct me to my next 'assignment'. It was during this time that I discovered a university that is well known for educating champions for Christ. I had never heard of the university prior to the very disappointing theatrics with my 'Christian' university.

I must share that it is amazing what I have been recalling as I write a number of these testimonies. I share such because I 'just' recalled that before joining the university, I was told by the previous professor, who did not know that I was a Christian, "don't trust the people who work at that school...even though it is considered a Christian university, it is nothing Christian about it." I took it as a grain of salt and thought that this professor was simply bitter about his departure. Well, during the five years or working there, and especially near the end, he was absolutely right.

The above is why I thoroughly researched Truly Christ-Centered University (TCCU). I discussed that TCCU's vision was to *educate twenty-first-century leaders for Korea and the world who embody excellence in both academics and Christian moral character, in particular, honesty and integrity*. My heart, mind, and spirit, leaped for joy and I proceeded to apply for the position at TCCU.

I even went as far as calling the director of the department in order to inform him that I was excited about the opportunity and it would be a perfect position for me. During that time, I was also contacted by another university, Nineveh University (NU) located in a different region, actually, right by the sea. Their vision statement was nothing like TCCU. Actually, they described their logo to be one that was designed to be a horned animal with a body like a deer, head similar to a dragon, feet resembling a horse, and a tail like a cow. I said out-loud... *Nooooooooo*! But, I could not shake the fact that I was supposed to go to the interview.

Prior to going to the interview, I exchanged a number of emails with the administration of NU. They were very professional and polite. They even paid for my transportation to the interview, which was something unexpected.

During the interview in front of four professors, including the head professor, I was asked, "Why did you come to South Korea?" Like hundreds of other times, I asked, "Do you want the long story or the short story? Regardless of which you pick, in the end, you might think I am crazy." I proceeded to tell them how God brought me to Korea. How I gave up everything in America because God told me that South Korea was my new home. They were all silent for some time and at the end of the story, they all just stared at me. After a few other questions, the interview ended and the head professor drove me back to the train station. I was 100% sure that I was not going to be offered the position, and I was okay with that. However, a few hours later, I was told that the job was mine and they wanted to know if I would say "Yes" to their offer.

A month earlier, I had no position, but at this point in time, I had three universities to choose from. Which choice should I make? Actually, for me, there wasn't a choice, I was 'definitely' going to work with the Christian university, TCCU. Everything about the university sounded perfect. Even after the phone interview with three of their professors, my heart, was set on serving at the university. But then... well, you know how it goes. God intervened.

I had a dream. In the dream there were two groups of people. I could not see their faces, but I was standing with one group that was shining brighter than white, due to the intense light shining from them and around them. Then there was another group, the people were darker than dark, because of the darkness that was coming out of them was also surrounding them. I was standing with the group surrounded by light while also looking at these two groups of people from up in the sky. Then suddenly, God reached down, picked me up out of the group with the light, and placed me in the group that was dark. Even before waking up, I knew that God was 'picking me up and putting me' in NU.

Even with all the years of obeying God, going where He wanted me to go, doing what He wanted me to do, I had a bad attitude about this one... a really bad attitude. This was the first time, in all my years walking with Him that I actually was upset about having to go into the darkness.

I was tired of all of what had been going on in my personal life as well as dealing with very traumatic issues that family and friends were going through as well. In addition, having to deal with people who did not want the best for me, generated a number of demonic experiences associated with them, and yet, God said, "Love them anyway!" Which I realized was easy for me to do from a distance, but when they were in my home or part of my inner-circle, walking away from them isn't as easy as dealing with someone you don't know very well.

I had reasoned in my own mind that I was done with giving time and effort to what we would call 'frenemies', which are people who appear to be your friend but secretly, and a lot of times, spiritually behave as an enemy. They do not celebrate your successes, nor do they get excited about the things that God is doing in your life. They are happiest and always around when things are going bad, but when God is blessing you financially, or professionally, they seem to be the ones against you.

Most Christians can fully quote, Ephesian 6:11-13, however, I had spent 10 years learning how to address the spiritual aspect of those who continuously welcomed the 'enemy' into their lives and proceed not to only cause destruction in others' lives, but self-destruct as well.

> *"Put on the full armor of God, so that you will be able to stand firm against the schemes of the devil. For our struggle is not against flesh and blood, but against the rulers, against the powers, against the world forces of this darkness, against the spiritual forces of wickedness in the heavenly places. Therefore, take up the full armor of God, so that you will be able to resist in the evil day, and having done everything, to stand firm.." (Ephesians 6:11-13 NIV).*

I was at a point where I just wanted to be around people who had the same heart towards God, wanted to help prepare champions for Christ, and simply contribute to advancing God's kingdom for His glory. But, God said, "Not now" as it related to working with TCCU. Given such, after passing through the third phase, of a five-phase interview process, which included a 62 page application, I sent the following email:

Dear Director Hope,

Since I have been saved, God has consistently made it absolutely clear as it relates to where I am supposed to go, may it be another country for missions, to where I am supposed to work. As of now, I still do not have a place of employment, being that X University is not renewing my contract and has dissolved my department. In addition, as I had shared before, I have turned down the other offers that were made at the beginning of the month. Again, no other university that was offering me a position sat well with me. Simply put, regardless of the salary, I simply did not have peace about them.

You must know that prior to our call, starting from the day I saw the advertisement for the position and while completing the....errhhmmmm 66-page application, I was running and jumping around with excitement at the possibility of actually working at a school where the faculty truly LOVES JESUS!!! After watching your YouTube video on 'Purity' and another professor's video on 'Evangelism', I thought, "Thank You Lord, a university in South Korea where they are kingdom focused and are actively equipping the next generation with what counts the most."

During this process, the process of completing TCCU's application and getting all of the references that were associated with the application, I continuously prayed, "God if this is for me...open the door wide, if it is not close it. If I am the perfect person that TCCU's needs at this point in time, please ensure that I do all that is required to honor their process of selection, and if I am not the perfect person for TCCU, let that be known as well."

However, since arriving to the states and talking/praying about all that is transpiring in Korea with finding an assignment...not a 'job' but an assignment, I am no longer 100% sure that I am supposed to work at TCCU 'at this point in time'. Please allow me to explain.

As I was sharing all that is happening in Korea, as well as with the various mission's organizations I work with, and along with the one that I and four friends have started, I feel like I am supposed to work 'with' TCCU in order to help you all with something that TCCU needs, versus working at TCCU. I am not sure if it is as someone coming in and doing some training for the staff and/or students, or helping set up the CALL systems that were discussed earlier, or joining you all for special seminars, etc.

To be honest, I am really not sure Professor Hope, but I do not feel/think that the timing is right for me to join TCCU as a faculty member. I do believe that I am to work at TCCU at some point in time, if the opportunity ever presents itself again... but I get the impression that it will be in another few years being that South Korea is where I will be for quite some time. Of course I could be wrong, however in the years of going where God says to go, and doing what He says to do, I believe at this point in time, it is not my time to work at TCCU.

Given the above, and in order for you all to focus on the remaining candidates who are full heartedly desiring to work with TCCU, I am presenting this email as my notice to withdraw from the pool of applicants. I would rather withdraw now, versus going through all of the interviews and waiting till the last minute to inform you of the above.

Again, I do hope that if another opportunity presents itself to 'join' TCCU, I pray that it will be God's timing for me. And, if you believe that there is something that I can help TCCU with at any point in time in the near future, please do not hesitate to let me know.

I honestly wanted to cry after sending the email. Pretty much act like a three-year-old and throw a temper tantrum, but I knew that I was not supposed to join TCCU because God had assigned me to Nineveh University.

The situation made me realize that, after all the years of traveling internationally for ministry, sometimes to three or four countries a year, and sometimes in one month, while not only working in universities in Korea, but also in America, I became all too familiar, and accustomed to engaging people and various spiritual situations where it all was becoming *routine.* Was it all still exciting? "Yes!" Was my heart still loving God and wanting to share Him with the world? "Yes!" However, He knew something about the position of my heart that I wasn't aware of, until my first week in Nineveh, South Korea.

After taking a week or so to process all that I saw taking place in Ninevah, I had resolved in my heart that if people wanted to serve the demonic by engaging in cultural witchcraft practices, they were more than free to do so. If they wanted to batter their bodies with alcohol and sex, while also abusing their spouses and children, I was not going to interfere. I had spent years attempting to get people to see that the life they were living was 'not' Korean culture. That is was not 'okay', and that I would never accept it.

I became fine with working, going to church, going home, and simply engaging those that God brought directly to me, versus, going out and seeking those who needed Him. I realized that the position of my heart was the results of a successful attack of the enemy. One that I have seen the enemy use on so many other people. I will call it *developing a stance of 'passive engagement'.*

Passive engagement is different for everyone. No one in my immediate circle of friends or family would ever be able to determine the position of my heart and mind when it came to going after, and loving the lost, however, God knew.

Did I still cry and grieve over Korean students who I knew were alcoholics or on their way to being alcoholics? Yes of course. Did I still pray for students whose household consisted of abusive parents or individuals who were involved in prostitution? Most definitely! But what I did not realize and only the Holy Spirit could show me, was that I did not engage the way I did previously, because I was tired of *'feeling'* and believing the lie that what God had me doing, wasn't making a difference.

I simply got tired of having the most illogical discussions with Koreans who told me that getting drunk was part of their culture. Being drunk and throwing up on the street or all over oneself was meant to be "freeing." That women and men, young and old, had the right to sell their bodies if they wanted to, or have sex with as many people they wanted. And, the comments that still make me shake my head the most, "lying, deception, and witchcraft 'should' be used in order to make sure you get what you need from people."

The problem with all of this was, it wasn't just coming from non-Christian, I was engaging in these conversations with people in church. With individuals who were ministers and even scarier, Korean missionaries who had traveled extensively to other nations.

Before moving on, I must address potential comments and arguments concerning my pointing out what is happening in South Korea. First, it is my story of what has happened, and still happening in a nation I so deeply love with every part of my being. I do not, and will never ignore the fact that the same, aforementioned issues are prevalent in other countries. However, there are rebuttals that people have consistently given me when I pointed out societal issues that need to change. "Well this happens in other countries, not just South Korea." "Why are you only talking about negative things in South Korea?" And, one that makes me cringe and grieves my very soul even more because I cannot count the amount of times I have heard it, "It is none of my business if my neighbor is beating his wife, or his children, he has the right to rule his house the way he wants to."

Using an argument that basically appeals to tradition, or only engaging in observational selection, which is basically, pointing out favorable circumstances while ignoring the unfavorable ones, will keep South Korea in a position where they will continue to have the highest rates of suicides out of all the OECD nations for the past decade.[30]

---

[30]South Korea's suicide rate remained highest among members of the Organization for Economic Cooperation and Development, while its health status was among the lowest, a recent OECD data showed. According to the 2015 Health Statistics report, issues by the OECD, an average of 29.1 people per 100,000 committed suicide in 2012, about 2 1/2 times the OECD average of 11.9, based on data compiled for 25 of 34 OECD members in the same year. The high rate of suicide

Despite the economic growth, the accolades received from around the world concerning their academic institutions, only the love of God, the knowledge of who He created them to be, and receiving His love, will change this nation.

Do all Koreans feel as though the state of their nation should be ignored? Of course not. I have not only met individuals who are crying out to God for their country, but given the fact that I do not speak the language fluently, I cannot fully engage in dialogue with thousands of people on the issues. However, the Koreans I have met, who do discuss these issues, are often persecuted and ridiculed at a level that I will not have to contend with. I have often said that Koreans who want their nation to change for the better will always have a harder time than a foreigner who desires change.

There are a number of reasons that Koreans will have a more challenging time than I. But the main reason is that a Korean who is speaking against anything associated with his or her country is automatically seen as a traitor and a detractor. For them to speak out against something that someone is doing, they could be charged with a crime and sentenced to prison or have a fee imposed.

For example, according to Article 311 of the South Korea Criminal Act, a person who publicly insults another shall be punished by imprisonment or imprisonment without prison labor for no more than one year or pay a fine not exceeding two million won. This is known as a crime of 'Insult'. This type of crime differs from defamation in that it deals with opinions, and not allegations of facts. Currently, the most common form of this crime is online name-calling. There is no separate "cyber" form of this crime, so Article 311 applies to both online and offline content. In addition, a criminal complaint is required in order to prosecute someone for the crime of 'Insult'.[31]

---

for Koreans is most apparent among students and the elderly. The country also ranked near the bottom in various criteria associated with their quality of life. (2015 Organization for Economic Co-operation and Development: Better Life Index) http://www.oecdbetterlifeindex.org/countries/korea/

[31]In chapter XXXIII Crimes Again Reputation, Article 309 of the Korean Criminal Act, states that a person who commits the crime of defamation by means of newspaper, magazine, radio, or other publication shall be punished. Article 311 of

Somewhere along the way, I fell into the lie believing that if Koreans were fighting to stay bound in darkness, by defending their culture, why should I continue to fight by sharing the truth, which is a natural approach, or with prayer, which is a spiritual approach? I knew with the new assignment in Nineveh, my thought process was going to change, and change quickly.

---

the Korean Criminal Act also states that a person who publicly insults another shall be punished.
http://elaw.klri.re.kr/eng_service/lawView.do?hseq=28627&lang=ENG

Abundance and Warfare

Most would think that one would be excited to be making more money than they had been making in previous years. It would be considered a promotion due to the fact that the job still required less hours of work per week, four additional weeks of vacation time, and yet, there I was, with a 'bad attitude', knowing that the assignment that God was sending me on was one that was going to be challenging on various levels.

After having a dear Korean friend, whose family is the personification of God's love and kindness, help me move to Nineveh, I unpacked, cleaned, and prayed up and out my apartment and the building complex. While taking a walk to the main street, I could not for the life of me understand why it felt like I was walking up hill and through pudding. I thought, maybe the area was situated on a hill. But even as I reached the main street, it felt as though I was pushing against a force that I could not see.

The first few days of classes were chaotic. Those of you who have worked in South Korea, within academia know exactly what I am talking about. For those who have never engaged in the rigmarole of the preposterous antics, I will not even begin to explain them, because you would simply not believe me. Actually, you would most likely believe my testimonies about angels and demons, before believing me about working in the university system.

After my first week of classes, I honestly thought that I was tricked by the devil. Please hear my heart as I share this, and it is not a gross exaggeration. About 95% of all of my students were dealing with depression, suicidal thoughts, schizophrenia, suffering from delusions, and living in a false reality. I honestly felt like the entire department was waiting to yell, "Surprise, it's all a joke!" That would be the end of the various events that were taking place, but I was wrong, "surprise" never came, and for 16 weeks, I dealt with students in my office breaking down into tears, wanting to drop out of school or commit suicide.

During my third week I met an American man, who was married to a Korean women, who had lived in the area for close to 15 years. He also used to be a pastor. He explained to me that the region was in fact known for having the highest concentration of shamans (Korean witchdoctors) and cults given the number of mountains in the region. I also found out that a lot of the businesses, restaurants, and a host of other enterprises were associated with the cults or false religions in the area.

While he shared this information, all I could think of was the one person who I had tried to help for years escape from the demonic terror of their parents who were part of one of the largest Korean cults in California. This person was tormented day and night, walked in a disillusioned state of reality, and refused to listen to people who God would send, from around the world, in order to speak truth to them. Now, there I was with close to 160 students who had similar, or the exact same issues. I was prepared to help and love the students as needed, however, what I wasn't prepared for were the professors who knew about the issues but made statements such as "It's not our problem." Along with a host of other unbelievable comments in response to all that was going on.

More money, more responsibility, definitely a promotion in the natural and spiritual realm, but how does one stay focused on God and His leading in order to obey Him, while knowing in your innermost being that you simply want to give up? One word, *'love'*.

During my first three months of arriving in South Korea, I cried almost every day. I could not gather my wits and emotions given the degradation in mindsets of students, as well as other young people I encountered on a daily basis.

I had girls that I knew were sexually active, and some of them did not want to be. I had to kick guys out of the classrooms because they came in either drunk or had hangovers from the night before. I had to also shoo away perverted older, foreign teachers who were looking at, and approaching the girls in a way that made the girls uncomfortable. And, I had to deal with individuals in the church body, who did not feel the need to pray or engage the issues.

I had to hold tight to the prophetic words that I received from a Korean pastor that I met in the states prior to moving to South Korea. "God is sending you to South Korea in order to show the love of the Father for those who are fatherless." I had received the same prophetic word five more times before leaving the United States. I knew God was making sure that I knew that I would be engaging those who did not feel loved and were doing everything in their power to fill the void of not having love.

During my first year in South Korea, I developed relationships with students, young and old, (my students ranged between 18-50 years of age) where I was the one they called when they got into trouble.

They all knew my story as it related to God bringing me to Korea. They also knew that I would never invite them to church. I told them that I did not believe in God prior to meeting Jesus Christ. I also shared with them that I could not understand why a good God would cause or allow so much pain, which was something that most of the people I talked to wanted to discuss. I also realized that this one issue, which most people wanted to receive an answer for, was due to the fact that they were in pain. However, I shared the gospel of Jesus Christ, with the understanding that it put them on the road to 'encounter Him' for themselves.

During these meetings there was always a lot of crying, and at times, a lot of anger and confusion once I helped them to realize why they were dealing with the various mental issues that brought them to meet with me. I made sure I did not use 'Christianeez' (words, or saying that only Christian people would understand), because they would not understand. However, I did make sure that they knew that they were loved by God and by me. Not because I was their professor or because as a Christian I am commanded to love. *I made sure that they understood, to the best of their cognitive abilities that I loved them because they were a representative of God's image here on earth, regardless of whether they believed it or not.* This is what was needed at Nineveh University, and this is what God had equipped me...for six years to do.

You see, engaging students at a Christian university did not mean that they were all Christian. Some made sure that I knew that they wanted nothing to do with Christianity even though they were at a Christian university in order to partake in the different educational programs that the school was known for. Even though they did not want anything to do with Christianity, the mere fact that they attended the university brought them under the covering of the prayers of the missionaries and Christians who had been praying for the schools since the early1950s.

However, NU students wanted absolutely nothing to do with God. The region they live in is considered one of the most economically wealthy areas in the country, and most of the students come from very wealthy families. Think of it this way, for those of you who know Rodeo Drive in the United States, Bond Street in London, or Canton Road in Hong Kong, you can easily see the wealth, and unfortunately, some of the attitudes that come with it. Was every student wealthy? Of course not, but there was a clear divide between those who were, and those who were not.

While answering many student's questions concerning why I came to South Korea, some students made it clear that I should not share my testimonies about Jesus Christ, even though He was the one who brought me to Korea. And even though the faculty knew that I was a Christian, I was informed on more than one occasion that I needed to take part in activities that were associated with lying, manipulation and one occasion theft. YES...THEFT.

Every week was a 'real battle', both in the natural and spiritual realm. Spiritually, the witches astral projecting into the classroom or even jumping out at me while I walked by students in the university's courtyards became a regular occurrence. It took about a week, or so for me to shine up my combat boots and get to 'loving'. And once I mastered one level, it was as if reinforcements were called into take me to an even higher level in God's desire to love.

After about a month of serious spiritual warfare I knew that God was winning when Korean people started to openly curse me. I will 'never' forget the day that I had scheduled to meet two professors in order to address *their* problem with a student's article about a number of students being bullied by the *President of the Student Body*. I will not go into the details here, but one professor bullied the other professor in order to prevent the student's paper from being published.

An hour before the meeting I walked to a store that was across the street from the campus in order to buy a bottle of water. While walking back to my building a Korean woman, while flailing her arms, growling, spitting, and yelling opened up a barrage of curses towards me. It was all in Korean. As I stopped and turned towards her, I began to respond with, "Jesus Christ is Lord and He loves you," with the biggest smile on my face. As I stood my ground facing her, repeating, "Jesus Christ is Lord and He loves you," the louder and angrier she became. The one thing I will never forget was the darkness around her was swelling to a point where I could hardly see her… in the natural. I must admit, it wasn't until I just wrote the above, that I realized it was a natural manifestation of the dream I had where people were surrounded by darkness.

I won't go into all the details of all that transpired during my nine months at NU, but I will share that students were delivered, some were set free, and some started their own journey searching for freedom and love. I also told them that given the fact that 'no one' could assemble enough information to convince me that Jesus Christ was real, they should not let anyone bully them into believing either. However, when they 'meet' Jesus, they will have an opportunity to say 'Yes' or 'No' to Jesus being their Lord and Savior.

We Obey Because We Love

Jesus, the Way to the Father

"Don't let your hearts be troubled. Trust in God, and trust also in me. 2 There is more than enough room in my Father's home. If this were not so, would I have told you that I am going to prepare a place for you? 3 When everything is ready, I will come and get you, so that you will always be with me where I am. 4 And you know the way to where I am going." 5 "No, we don't know, Lord," Thomas said. "We have no idea where you are going, so how can we know the way?"

6 Jesus told him, "I am the way, the truth, and the life. No one can come to the Father except through me. 7 If you had really known me, you would know who my Father is. From now on, you do know him and have seen him!"

8 Philip said, "Lord, show us the Father, and we will be satisfied."

9 Jesus replied, "Have I been with you all this time, Philip, and yet you still don't know who I am? Anyone who has seen me has seen the Father! So why are you asking me to show him to you? 10 Don't you believe that I am in the Father and the Father is in me? The words I speak are not my own, but my Father who lives in me does his work through me. 11 Just believe that I am in the Father and the Father is in me. Or at least believe because of the work you have seen me do.

12 "I tell you the truth, anyone who believes in me will do the same works I have done, and even greater works, because I am going to be with the Father. 13 You can ask for anything in my name, and I will do it, so that the Son can bring glory to the Father. 14 Yes, ask me for anything in my name, and I will do it!

Jesus Promises the Holy Spirit

15 "If you love me, obey my commandments. 16 And I will ask the Father, and he will give you another Advocate, who will never leave you. 17 He is the Holy Spirit, who leads into all truth. The world cannot receive him, because it isn't looking

for him and doesn't recognize him. But you know him, because he lives with you now and later will be in you. 18 No, I will not abandon you as orphans—I will come to you.

19 Soon the world will no longer see me, but you will see me. Since I live, you also will live. 20 When I am raised to life again, you will know that I am in my Father, and you are in me, and I am in you. 21 Those who accept my commandments and obey them are the ones who love me. And because they love me, my Father will love them. And I will love them and reveal myself to each of them."

22 Judas (not Judas Iscariot, but the other disciple with that name) said to him, "Lord, why are you going to reveal yourself only to us and not to the world at large?"

23 Jesus replied, "All who love me will do what I say. My Father will love them, and we will come and make our home with each of them. 24 Anyone who doesn't love me will not obey me. And remember, my words are not my own. What I am telling you is from the Father who sent me. 25 I am telling you these things now while I am still with you. 26 But when the Father sends the Advocate as my representative—that is, the Holy Spirit—he will teach you everything and will remind you of everything I have told you.

27 "I am leaving you with a gift—peace of mind and heart. And the peace I give is a gift the world cannot give. So don't be troubled or afraid. 28 Remember what I told you: I am going away, but I will come back to you again. If you really loved me, you would be happy that I am going to the Father, who is greater than I am. 29 I have told you these things before they happen so that when they do happen, you will believe.

30 I don't have much more time to talk to you, because the ruler of this world approaches. He has no power over me, 31 but I will do what the Father requires of me, so that the world will know that I love the Father. Come, let's be going. (John 14)

A Heart of Obedience

After living over a decade of loving God and allowing Him to love me, I came to better understand why *obedience is better than sacrifice.*

When we read the various stories in the Bible about people 'doing' things that looked good, like sacrificing animals, we first must study and realize that animal sacrifices in the Old Testament were not simply performed by Israelites. Ancient Near Eastern people sacrificed animals as a way of appeasing their gods. In any case, God required the Israelites to sacrifice animals in order to remember the death consequences of sin and to therefore repent when they'd broken covenant with God.

However, we can see that in Israel's history, people began sacrificing animals without repenting in their heart. The Lord told them (through prophets like Isaiah, Hosea and Amos) that He despised their sacrifices, for they were meaningless without a change in heart.

"The sacrifice of the wicked is detestable-- how much more so when brought with evil intent!" (Proverbs 21:27)

"Stop bringing meaningless offerings! Your incense is detestable to me. New Moons, Sabbaths and convocations-- I cannot bear your worthless assemblies." (Isaiah 1:13)

"...a people who continually provoke me to my very face, offering sacrifices in gardens and burning incense on altars of brick;..." (Isaiah 65:3)

"...who sit among the graves and spend their nights keeping secret vigil; who eat the flesh of pigs, and whose pots hold broth of impure meat;.." (Isaiah 65:4)

"What do I care about incense from Sheba or sweet calamus from a distant land? Your burnt offerings are not acceptable; your sacrifices do not please me." (Jeremiah 6:20)

"I hate, I despise your religious festivals; your assemblies are a stench to me." (Amos 5:21)

"Even though you bring me burnt offerings and grain offerings, I will not accept them. Though you bring choice fellowship offerings, I will have no regard for them." (Amos 5:22)

Or even the story of the Rich Young Ruler in the New Testament, God wants our heart to be open and willing to surrender to His ways.

The Rich and the Kingdom of God

17 As Jesus started on his way, a man ran up to him and fell on his knees before him. "Good teacher," he asked, *"what must I do to inherit eternal life?"*

18 "Why do you call me good?" Jesus answered. "No one is good—except God alone. 19 You know the commandments: 'You shall not murder, you shall not commit adultery, you shall not steal, you shall not give false testimony, you shall not defraud, honor your father and mother.'

20 "Teacher," he declared, "all these I have kept since I was a boy." 21 Jesus looked at him and loved him. "One thing you lack," he said. "Go, sell everything you have and give to the poor, and you will have treasure in heaven. Then come, follow me." 22 At this the man's face fell. He went away sad, because he had great wealth. (Matthew 19:17-22)

It is clear with these scriptures as well as hundreds of others, that God desires us to have a heart solely focused on Him. We should not actively engage in activities that make us 'appear' that our heart is worshiping and loving Him, when in actuality it is not. Even if we are giving away all that we have, traveling to where He tells us to travel, or doing, and even saying all that He requires us to do or say, it is not glorifying Him, nor is He pleased with it. He desires for us to be in complete agreement in our heart and mind with Him and only Him.

Even after all of the traveling, giving, and doing, I realized that God was letting me know that I started operating, at some point in time, on auto-pilot with being obedient. There was, and will always be a higher realm of revelation concerning loving and obeying Him, that I need(ed) to be ushered into. But, I found out that in order to 'level up', I had to ensure that I did not have a 'heart attitude' that had residue of hurt, or even offense that would keep me from growing in a deeper relationship with Him and the people I encountered.

A lot of times, we don't realize that we can be offended towards God, especially if we get busy with going, doing, and even worshiping him. But because He is so very gracious and loving, and wants us to worship Him in spirit and 'His Truth', His love lets us know when there is a place in our heart that needs to be surrendered to Him so that we can move higher in Him. It is not that we are, 'not high' in Him. It is more of having revelation of where we are in Him.

One day while sitting in church, after traveling for three months throughout various parts of Asia, seeing the most amazing miracles, and seeing people receive the love of Jesus, an overwhelming feeling of loneliness and fear came over me. I began to weep while singing... "I will go to where you need me..." As I wept, I asked the Lord, why was I feeling so much sorrow?

The thoughts that came were, God you have sent me around the world, you are still sending me around the world, but I no longer want to go 'alone'. Even though I was going with teams of people, I wanted to go with my spouse, my husband. At that point in time, I realized that I wanted to married. There were a lot of people that I was surrounded by who strongly desired to be married, but I did not seem to desire it as strongly as them. I was okay loving God alone, and having Him love me.

As these thoughts became stronger, I could not understand why, because I had the thoughts before with no emotions tied to them, at least not like what I was experiencing. As the service started, a couple who God was sending to another country came to give their testimony. They shared what God was doing in their marriage and what God was going to be using them to do in another country they would be ministering in.

The next day, God told me to go to another country. Once I booked my ticket, I began to ask God, why He wanted me to go back to this specific country because I had just been there a few months earlier. I discovered that there was a ministry associated with ending the sex trade that the country is known for. The ministry actively goes into the brothels, the red light districts, and pull people, women, men, and children off the streets, and take them through a process of restoration.

As I reviewed their website, I began to get excited along with what can best be described as butterflies in my stomach. I knew that I was going to do anything and everything the ministry needed. From cleaning the facilities, to joining them during their night out-reaches for lost souls, I was prepared to serve in any capacity that was needed.

As I prayed for the ministry, God gave me revelation as to what was happening to me the day before. If I had not surrendered, fully surrendered my desires to be married, to have a family, and travel the world with my husband ministering the gospel, I do not believe that I would have been given the opportunity to go and serve in the nation I was being sent to.

I have often wondered why so many men and women have fallen, even with their huge ministries and amazing display of God's power. I now understand that there are a plethora of reasons for which at this point in time I will not be addressing. However, what came to me was the realization that the spirit of offense against God can keep you from walking in all that He has called you to do, but more importantly become.

I have read and heard a number of stories about those who had given their lives to serve God's people and reach the lost, and yet, lived with the belief that they had to give up everything they desired for themselves. Even giving up everything they 'believed' they needed in order to go and accomplish everything that God was requiring them to do.

So they went and served around the world. Pleasing God, and sometimes falling into the sin of pleasing people. But hidden in the deepest areas of their heart are those unmet needs that have yet to manifest. May it be a spouse, salvation for family members, financial or healing needs, that have yet to be met...the enemy brought those reminders to them. I have since learned that if one doesn't rebuke those lies, or allow God to ensure that they don't influence ones heart towards Him, one will not finish well.

If *we* are not diligent in allowing the Holy Spirit to show us our heart on a regular basis, we will bury them deep in our mind and heart, and they will start to turn into bitterness and envy against the people that God has called us to serve.

I had often wondered how and why people were so very angry and bitter, even though they have 'worked' in ministry for 20, 30, and sometimes 40 years. They still exegete and pontificated scriptures that keeps their congregation growing and engaged. They could still prophesy and lay hands on the sick, where people are healed, and yet, they were so very mean to those closest to them. It is because they have allowed the calcification of the lies that God was 'using them' instead of being used by God, to cloak their mind and heart.

If I allowed what the enemy was whispering to me during that service, to be embedded in my heart and mind, that God 'was not going to fulfill His promises to me', then why would God continue to give me assignments where my physical body was obeying him, but my heart was not? Remember, "*half-hearted obedience or delayed obedience is clocked rebellion.*"

I realized that yes, you can go and have huge crusade, have healing conferences, minister where the Holy Spirit moves and people's lives are changed, but then go back to your room and cry your eyes out. Why, because the enemy whispers, "Yes they received all that they needed, but you STILL have not."

What also came to mind was when the devil went to God and talked about Job. I believe that while sitting in church, the enemy wanted to see if I would be offended towards God, and seek what I wanted first, before seeking the things of God. And, as I sit here, typing this out, I have consistently vowed, that I will never put anyone or anything, or even better, any of God's promises above what God has called me to do, which is to love Him with all my heart, mind, and strength.

I am still waiting to see my own family members, co-workers, and acquaintances saved and set free. Yet, I will go and be an instrument of God to those He desires to heal and set free. I am still waiting to meet a man who fears and loves God first, loves himself, and loves people. But while I wait, I still pray for married couples who are struggling and buy wedding dresses for friends, and even strangers who are getting married. I am still waiting for my student loans to be paid off, but I will still contribute to the building of schools, hospitals, and to the development of nations around the world. I will cheerfully sow as He tells me to sow, and give all that He asks me to give.

While it appears to be easy for some, and challenging for most to walk completely in obedience to all that God calls one to do, even though it all sounds illogical, people need to simply ask themselves, do they 'really' love God.

Years ago, I would have stated that one should ask, are they 'really' saved, because how does one proclaim to know the One who gave them life, and say they are saved, but their lives looks nothing like the life of the God they say they serve? If we are indeed saved, then we must actually 'live' like it, not act like it, as in the falsities we find in entertainment, or in the instances when we encounter people who are engaging us out of hidden motives that are eventually discovered.

If we proclaim our existence is due to God, it should involve love towards all, while knowing that God's love is not adjusting and agreeing with sin. And, it has nothing to do with letting people who believe lies continue to believe them.

Hearing and walking out truth is not the mere acknowledgment and understanding of facts. Most people believe that facts are *truths*. But in actuality, being that Christ is the 'Truth', what He says, what He has done, will do, and is doing, is truth. No matter how many people that want to deny the *Truth*, He continuously gives them opportunities for them to receive Him on this side of eternity. Whether it is on this side, or the other, every knee will bow, and every tongue will confess that Jesus Christ is Lord.

If you have read this entire book, or like some, who read the first and last pages in order to determine if you will give your time to go on the various journeys shared, it is my hope that you realize that you still have time, to acknowledge and receive Jesus Christ as your Lord and Savior.

After doing so, you, as well as all of us who say we love Him, must continue to grow in our understanding that our obedience to Jesus Christ is rewarded here on earth. Choosing to be obedient to love Him, love others, and follow Him is a unique feature of being alive. Think about it, once we die we will meet Him. For those of us who hear, "Well done my good and faithful servant", we will exist in eternity, worshiping the one we chose to live for while here on earth.

Obey Him on this side, because it is the only chance you will have. I pray that you will have revelation that it will be so very worth it in the end, because He is the only one worthy of our love and obedience.

Made in the USA
Coppell, TX
16 April 2021

53853367R00121